Faith is for People

Faith is for People

PAUL LITTLE

VISION HOUSE PUBLISHERS
Santa Ana, California 92705

Revised Standard Version Bible used by permission.

Faith Is for People

Copyright © 1976 by Vision House Publishers
Santa Ana, California 92705

Library of Congress Catalog Number 76-40714
ISBN 0-88449-057-2

Printed in the United States of America

CONTENTS

INTRODUCTION

Paul Little stands high in the ranks of Christian speakers and authors. In this outstanding book, published posthumously, the author makes us laugh, cry, and think. Most important of all, he shows us how totally logical and vital it is for all of us to place our entire faith squarely on Jesus Christ Himself.

As editor of the tape transcript on which this book is based, I can recommend every page as an enduring testimony to the familiar adage, "He, being dead, yet speaketh." May God speak to all of us through the enduring words of Paul E. Little.

—Raymond Schafer

1

WHAT'S WRONG WITH THE WORLD?

Some time ago a Mr. Fred Christianson was brutally beaten and killed in our northwest Chicago suburb by three teenagers who were under the influence of pep pills. Not only was Chicago shocked, but the whole nation was shocked as the story went out over the news wires. Thousands of people asked themselves "Why?" "Why would three affluent teenagers murder an innocent man?" And then we began to realize once more that this murder was merely a symptom of the malignant disease that is spreading throughout our society today—that there is something terribly, radically wrong with our modern America.

Not Just the Preachers

It's not just the religious leaders who are decrying these crimes, but the secular leaders of society as well. Some time ago J. Robert Moskin, the senior editor of *Look* magazine, wrote these words: "Most Americans hate to admit we are in a crisis, but its bitter fruits are all around us— the . . . racist, the wild kid, the price-rigging executive, the pregnant high school girl, the dope addict, the bribed athlete, the uncared-for aged, the poor, the criminal . . . . Television depicts shoot-em-up violence as the American way, and the movies uphold Steinem as a warrant for four husbands and a lover." This wasn't a religious prophet of doom—this was the senior editor of *Look* magazine as he looked out over America today.

But the problem doesn't stop with our own United States, with our own communities. Thoughtful people all over the world are coming to realize that we're facing a tremendous world-wide crisis. Among other things, the advent of "the bomb" has radically changed life's outlook for everybody. The late President Kennedy observed before his death that mankind is now facing its greatest crisis in history. Red China's recent underground nuclear explosions have only aggravated people's fears as they look out over the world with its imminent possibility of nuclear destruction.

Where Have We Gone Wrong?

Everyone agrees that there is something wrong with the world, but the $64,000 question is, exactly what is the cause for the problem? What is it that makes us victims of this kind of haunting fear? What is it that plagues this age of unprecedented technological progress—more progress than in any other age of history—with such flagrant problems? Whatever our exact point of view, I think we would all agree that, before we can ever arrive at a workable solution to any particular problem, we first need to come up with an accurate diagnosis of that problem. Bona fide cures are always directly related to accurate diagnoses.

If I had a stomachache tonight and somebody diagnosed me as having indigestion and gave me Pepto Bismol, whereas in point of fact I happened to have acute appendicitis, I'd be in pretty grim shape by tomorrow morning! If the cure isn't related to an accurate diagnosis, it's just a worthless cure. On the other hand, if all I had was indigestion and some eager surgeon took my appendix out, that wouldn't be particularly helpful either! It might relieve me from possible problems later on, but it wouldn't be the solution to my immediate problem, which could have been taken care of with Pepto Bismol. Diagnosis and cure go hand in hand. Unless we have an accurate dignosis initially, we are not going to come up with a dynamic solution that is workable or makes sense. It's very interesting to notice that in the twentieth century three major diagnoses of the world's problems have been advanced, along with corollary solutions by thinkers of our time. Let's consider these three major diagnoses in the next few pages.

Peace Through Education?

One diagnosis of the world's problems that has been very widely held, particularly before World War II, is that the basic problem of the human race is mostly ignorance, and that the solution to the problems of the world and of mankind could be achieved by universal education. H. G. Wells, the noted British philosopher and historian, propounded this view as one of its most vocal adherents. According to this view, man is basically good and perfectable, and all that is required to fully perfect him is to educate the human race.

Now I'm sure none of us is against education. We all want as much education as we can get. But on closer analysis it would seem that this point of view is rather inadequate as a diagnosis of our situation. As a matter of fact Mr. Wells himself, over a period of years, came to the place of abandoning his own "educating" point of view. World War I came as somewhat of a shock to him as he saw nations becoming involved in an incredible holocaust, but he explained this slaughter (along with many other men at that time) as "the war to end all wars." Sure, man has slipped on the ladder of progress, but *now* we are finally ready to complete the program that we had begun to initiate before we were slowed up by this tragedy of World War I.

But only twenty years later World War II came along and, with a tremendous shock, buried World War I by comparison. Now it was becoming rather obvious that some of the most highly educated nations in the world were participating in some of the most incredible atrocities that mankind had ever known in history. In the stark reality of World War II and all its tragedy, H. G. Wells wrote a book in 1946 called *Mind at the End of Its Tether*, in which he came to the abysmal conclusion, "I have concluded that man is not worth educating." The sheer, overwhelming weight of the historical fact of World War II had completely shattered his optimistic opinion about human nature and its perfectability, and, while Wells still believed in education for certain purposes, he recognized that the problem of human nature lay much deeper than mere education.

Knowledge Is Not Virtue

A great many philosophers abandoned Wells' position even though they had been proponents

11

of it prior to World War II, and pessimism has now become the vogue in philosophical circles. This is probably best exemplified by Jean-Paul Sartre, the Nobel Prize winner, in his whole existentialist philosophy, which is in the forefront of people's thinking today in many parts of the world. Education can be useful, but if education were basically the solution to the human problem, we could expect to find that the university community (since it presumably has the greatest corner on knowledge and information) would be the most moral segment of any given society.

It has been my privilege, as some of you may know, to visit hundreds of university campuses all over the United States and in different countries around the world, and I'm afraid I would have to say, as much as I would like to think otherwise, that the university community is by no means the moral apex in any given society. In fact, it's often far from the top in that respect. The recent scandals at the military academies have shocked many of us into realizing that education in itself does not guarantee anything in terms of moral behavior—the working out of those things which we know to be right and true.

No, man's problem is not *knowing* what he ought to do. His basic problem is the moral power to *do* what he knows to be right. Everyone throughout the world agrees that war is wrong, but that doesn't stop war. Knowledge is not virtue in this sense. Knowledge is useful, but there is a problem that lies beyond it, and it would seem, surveying all the evidence, that C. S. Lewis, the late English literature critic and world-famous figure, was closer to the truth when he made the rather cryptic observation that education, as useful as it is, seems only to serve to make man a more clever devil. Education can be a useful thing, but in itself it doesn't solve the basic moral dilemma of the human race.

Peace for a Price?

The second diagnosis that has been advanced, one that is held by many people today as being the basic problem of the world, is that of poverty. As this thesis goes, everything is determined by economics, and the solution to the world's problem is essentially economic equality. Of course you will recognize immediately that this is one of the basic theses of one of the most widespread and widely followed philosophical and economic theories in the world today, dialectical Marxism. This is essentially its tenet—that everything is determined economically, and that we can solve the problem of humanity and the human race by bringing about economic equality.

All of us, I'm sure, will agree that every human

being should have enough food to eat, should have adequate clothing, should have housing and medical care, and so on, and that we should work to make this possible for people who do not have this privilege. Yet on closer analysis, as appealing as this diagnosis and its corollary solution initially appear to be, it would seem that the diagnosis is a rather superficial analysis of the human problem. The tragic fact is that our own country, the United States, bears eloquent testimony to the fact that economic prosperity is an inadequate diagnosis for the human dilemma and the problem of the human race.

The United States leads the world in economic standards. We have the greatest number of telephones, the greatest number of bathtubs, the greatest number of automobiles, the greatest number of television sets, and the highest per capita income in the world, but we also lead the world, unfortunately, in crime, in juvenile delinquency, and in divorce. It seems that economic affluence, as useful and helpful as it may be, and as much as all of us would like to have it, does not basically solve the primary problem of the human race and human nature. If we happen to know people with lots of money, we realize that many of them bear testimony to the fact that, as useful as money is and as much as we would all like to have more of it than we do, money in itself does not bring satisfaction to the people who have it.

The Anguish of Affluence

Some time ago we were shocked by the apparent suicide of the Zenith heir in Arizona. One of his friends reported that he had said shortly before his suicide that life had no meaning for him because he had so much money. For so many people in the world today, money represents all of life's meaning to them; they give their every ounce of energy to accumulate money. The tragedy of it all is that when you get money it's like a handful of fog—it doesn't satisfy that inner longing at all. Again, as useful as money is (none of us would turn down a legacy, I'm sure!), economic affluence does not solve the deep-seated problem of the world.

The secular analysis of this point of view is found in a careful study by two New York psychiatrists in a book called *The Split-Level Trap*. This book examines the people of a suburban county in northern New Jersey—people who have achieved more economic affluence than they had anticipated and as a result were suffering in their home life and their own personal lives. Though many of these people had looked to money as a source of satisfaction, meaning, and purpose in life, they found that this was not the case, and disillusionment set in despite the achievement of the economic goals toward which these people had worked so hard. So economic equality as the solution to the world's ills fails to really strike at the root of the problem.

Science to the Rescue?

The third diagnosis of the world's problems that has been advanced and is held in many quarters today is what we call technological lag. By this we mean the lag in the application of scientific methods to the social and human problems of the world. In this view, technological advance would be the basic solution to the problem. This thesis notes that we have made tremendous strides through science (and of course we have, and all of us are very grateful for the fruits of scientific research and dazzled by the space age in which we live), but the thesis adds that because we have had to devote much of our technological energies to defense, we have missed getting on top of these social problems by applying the scientific method to them. If only we would do this we would begin to find the way out of our dilemmas; the scientific method itself holds the solution to the basic problems of the human race.

But, again, thoughtful observers (including some of the leading scientists of our day) are beginning to recognize that, as tremendously useful as the scientific method is as a gateway to reality and discovery, and as tremendously blessed as we have been by the discovery of the fruits of scientific research and endeavor, there is nothing in the scientific method itself capable of giving moral direction to the discoveries that science makes. There is nothing within the scientific method itself that will decide whether the fruits of nuclear research will be used to destroy cities or to destroy cancer. This is a moral problem which lies beyond the question of science; it is a problem of man himself.

The Bomb Is Not to Blame

We don't really fear the H-bomb itself. It's the *men who have the H-bomb* whom we fear. In the hands of someone who is honest and just and loving and kind, the H-bomb is as harmless as a baby's rattle. In the hands of an unscrupulous person who would do anything to achieve power, it can become an instrument of world annihilation and something before which we tremble.

Erich Fromm, the great psychiatrist, said not long ago, "Technologically we're in the space age, emotionally we're in the stone age." The late Dr. Carl Compton, a prominent nuclear physicist, said shortly before he died, "Unless the human race experiences and achieves a moral and spiritual advance equal to the technological advance that it has made, we are on the verge of annihilation." He saw that, as useful and as wonderful as the scientific method is, it is of itself incapable of solving the basic human problem that everyone seems to be aware of but is not quite sure how to solve.

Now if you've been thinking through these solutions, I think you'll observe that each of them has one thing in common with each of the others, and that is that each solution is external to individual people. The whole question of universal education is something outside any particular person, and so is the whole question of economic equality and of technological research. Somehow individual people just don't appear to want to take the blame for the mess that the world is in.

2

THE ANSWER OF CHRIST

The one diagnosis of the world's problems that
appears to be most akin to human experience and
most realistic in terms of history as we have
surveyed it is a solution which was advanced
almost two thousand years ago by Jesus of
Nazareth. This point of view was advanced by
Jesus Christ in a conversation that He had with a
group of religious leaders who viewed the whole
human problem and the whole question of
religion and reality as something outside
individual people. These religious leaders were
called Pharisees, and as men who had
externalized the human problem and its solution,
they were very concerned with all kinds of
ceremonial formulas—how you washed your
hands or didn't wash them before you ate your
food, what utensils you used, and so on. But Jesus

Christ got into quite a conversation with these men one day, and in this conversation He put his finger on the heart of the human problem, pointing out to them that they had missed the boat completely by externalizing the problem.

That conversation, for those of you who may be interested in reading it, is recorded in the Gospel According to Mark, in verses 14 to 23 of chapter 7. Christ began His conversation by saying, "He called the people to him again and said to them, 'Hear me, all of you, and understand: there is nothing outside a man which, by going into him, can defile him, but the things which come out of a man are what defile him.' And when he had entered the house and left the people, his disciples asked him about the parable. And he said to them, 'Then are you also without understanding? Do you not see that whatever goes into a man from outside cannot defile him, since it enters not his heart but his stomach, and so passes on?' " (Mark 7:14-19 RSV).

It's Not What You Eat

Thus Jesus declared all foods clean. He said that what comes *out* of a man is what defiles him, for out of the heart of a man come evil thoughts, fornication, theft, murder, adultery, coveting, wickedness, deceit, licentiousness, an evil eye, slander, pride, and foolishness. All these evil things come *from within*, and it is these things that defile a man. Jesus Christ says, in other words, "You've missed the point completely—it's backwards from the way you think it is. The basic problem of the human race is not *outside* a man, but *internal*. It's inside a man. *This* is the thing that has caused his own problems and the world's problems. *This* is the thing that has defiled the human race." Jesus Christ said in effect, "This defilement has separated man from God, his Maker, and this is the basic problem of the human race and of individual human beings."

It's very interesting to note, in this listing of statements that Jesus Christ made in His conversation with religious leaders, that He discusses thoughts and actions almost in the same breath. He speaks of murder and hatred and impurity of thought. There are thoughts as well as actions in the categories which He lists here as evidence of man's basic problem. The reason for this, as we discover in other places in the New Testament and in other words by Jesus Christ, is that God thinks of us as human beings not only in terms of our *actions* but also in terms of our *attitudes*. The fact of the matter is that some of us have never done certain sinful things that other people have done (whom we look down upon and think ourselves superior to) simply because we have not been tempted in the same way that these people have. Yet if our thought life were to be exposed, if we were to be known as we really are inside, we would find ourselves in the same situation as any other sinners. Jesus Christ said that the basic problem of this kind of attitude is separation from God because of defilement.

God Is Holy

In other places Jesus explains that God is absolutely pure and holy in His character, and that just as light and darkness cannot coexist in the same place—since when light comes in it inherently destroys darkness—so the blazing purity of God is such that we cannot exist in the presence of God if we are defiled and separated from our Creator. *This* is the basic problem of the human race—separation from the God who created us. We the human race and we as individuals are separated from God by our sins. We have become alienated from the reality of God, and this is our continuing tragic problem.

It's interesting to discover a twentieth-century echo of this two-thousand-year-old diagnosis. A couple of years ago, author E. Stanley Jones sent his book on conversion to one of the leading psychiatrists in Europe, Carl Gustav Jung (one of the big three of Freud, Adler, and Jung). Jones wondered what kind of response he would get from this leading psychiatrist. Generally speaking, many psychiatrists have not been too sympathetic to a supernaturalistic or religious point of view. So Jones was quite astounded when he received a letter from Jung saying, "Those psychiatrists who are not superficial have come to the conclusion that the vast neurotic misery of the world could be termed a neurosis of emptiness. Men cut themselves from the root of their being, from God, and then life turns empty, inane, meaningless, without purpose, so when God goes, goal goes, when goal goes, meaning goes, when meaning goes, value goes, and life turns dead on our hands." That's an interesting echo, is it not, of this particular diagnosis that Jesus advanced some two thousand years ago as the basic problem of the human race?

My Sin

Now this internal condition that Jesus spoke about in His diagnosis of the human problem He calls sin. In our society today sin is not a word that communicates very well, because the minute you say the word "sin" the average person thinks of "My Sin" perfume or "Night-of-Sin" films with Brigitte Bardot. People usually associate sin with immorality, and if they don't happen to be immoral people they get highly incensed because they think the word doesn't apply to them.

But of course immorality is only one meaning of the word "sin" as used by Jesus Christ in relation to the human dilemma. Sin is essentially a disease of the human race. The symptoms vary from person to person, but the disease is universal to the human race. Every culture and every strata of society holds a self-centered and rebellious or indifferent attitude toward God, the Creator. If you think through the listing that Jesus Christ mentioned in His conversation with the religious leaders of His day, you discover something very interesting: the basic root of every listed sin is essentially self-centeredness.

The Big I

Basically, what are our problems in society today? Are they not self-centeredness magnified to communal, national, and international levels? What's the problem in a given house? Two people can't get along with each other—self-centeredness—and there's a clash. What happens when there's community tension? It's self-centeredness magnified a little further. What is it when nations conflict with each other? It's the self-centeredness of the group manifesting itself, and a struggle goes on as to which group will prevail. And what do we see on a very broad canvas in the United Nations? Every problem that comes before it is essentially an extrapolation of the self-centeredness that characterizes us as individuals. This should provide the clue that turns us toward Christ's diagnosis of the human dilemma—that the basic problem of the human race is that we have become separated from God through self-centeredness and rebellion against Him.

Think of ourselves for a moment, to use a mechanized illustration, as an automobile. God created us to function properly and in a way that would bring us the greatest happiness and enjoyment and meaning and purpose in a close relationship with Himself, a relationship in which He is in control of our lives, even as an automobile is constructed to function properly when there is an intelligent, sober driver behind the wheel. But if the driver takes the car to the top of a hill, gives the car a gentle shove, and then jumps out, what happens? That automobile careens wildly down the hill, caroming into this and crashing into that and ending up at the bottom of the hill in a mangled mess, and probably having wreaked lots of damage along the way. The car wasn't built to function this way. It was built to function properly with an intelligent, sober driver behind the wheel.

Man Away from God

As we read what Jesus Christ said throughout the rest of the Bible, we find that, in a sense, this is the way we are made in terms of our relationship to our Creator. He created us to find purpose and meaning in a particular relationship with Himself, in which *He* is in control of our lives, guiding us and directing us. But the first man rebelled against God and, so to speak, shoved God out of the driver's seat of his life. In a sense every one of us has ratified that decision, and this is what has caused our problem. We have become separated from God, our Creator. We're like a lamp that has the plug pulled out of the socket, cut off from the source of moral power, cut off from the dynamics that God intends us to have, separated from Him. We're victims of the universal disease of sin.

What are some of the other symptoms of this disease? Emptiness and meaninglessness, not really knowing or understanding what the whole rat race is all about, wondering how the whole thing fits together and what it's all leading to, frustration and loneliness in the midst of a teeming multitude of people. This is the "lonely crowd" idea that David Riesman, the Harvard sociologist, wrote about in his famous book. Another symptom of this desease is guilt. We find ourselves unable to shake off a guilt that is ours because of deliberate wrongdoing somewhere along the line. We have a lack of self-control; we grind our gears, wishing we could change our behavior patterns. We vow over and over that we will change, but we find that we are unable to change even though we want to very much. These are a few of the symptoms of this disease of sin that infects every one of us in the human race.

Am I Better than You?

But you may be thinking, do you mean to say that we're all in the same situation, that all of us are as bad as the three teenagers who murdered Mr. Christianson? No, that's obviously not the case. It becomes quite obvious, as we look around at people, that there is a vast difference in the quality of lives that men live. Some men live far better lives than others. The real problem lies in the eternal God's standard of infinite holiness and perfection. Because of God's perfect character, the only way we can be in dynamic relationship with Him is to be perfect ourselves. Yet measured against that standard every one of us has failed. We may be better than someone else, but unless we have absolute perfection we cannot make it in the terms that God has laid down, in the terms of God's own moral character.

Not long ago a commercial airliner crashed into a mountaintop while trying to land at Las Vegas in a snowstorm. The most tragic thing of all about the crash was that it occurred only a couple of feet from the top of the mountain. Another few feet and they'd have made it over the mountain, but all of those people were as dead as if they had crashed a thousand feet further down. If we think of this as a moral scale of people's lives, we recognize that though there may be great differences in morality, absolute perfection is the thing that is really necessary in God's sight.

Another suggestion is to think of Hawaii as representing God's standard of holiness and righteousness. Let us imagine lining up the whole human race on the west coast of California. Everyone's success or failure in swimming to Hawaii will be determined by the moral quality of the life he lives. Here is a very upstanding person in the community, yet one who would be the first to admit that he is imperfect. (The interesting thing is that the better a person is the more conscious he is of his own failure!) You've probably noticed this as one of the characteristics of a good person. Here he is 75 miles out and still churning. Then there are the Joe College types that I meet all over the place, just happy-go-lucky people not really bad enough for Alcatraz. They get smashed on the weekends and cheat on a few exams, but they're not ready for federal prison yet. They are, let's say, ten miles out. And then there are the derelicts from skid row, only five hundred yards offshore but practically drowning.

We All Fall Short

There's no comparison in the quality of lives that these people have lived, is there? There's a big difference between them. Yet in terms of the ultimate objective, Hawaii, they're all in exactly the same situation—far short of the goal. Every one of the swimmers needs something done for him that he cannot do for himself. The only way any of them is going to make it to Hawaii is if he is taken there in a boat or plane. Something must be done for him which he can't do for himself. This is essentially what Jesus Christ said about our life situation—that the basic problem of the human race is internal, that we are all suffering from a mortal disease which He calls sin and defines as essentially self-centeredness, separating us from God because of our indifference and rebellion against Him.

The wonderful thing about Jesus Christ is that He not only *diagnosed* the problem which has separated us from God, but He also gave us the dynamic *solution*. Many of our modern pundits consider themselves tremendous at diagnosis, but they are a little weak when it comes to effective prescription! But Jesus Christ put the two together, and of course His entire life and death and resurrection, as well as much of the New Testament, is taken up with the explanation of that diagnosis.

The True Solution

He Himself, Christ said, was the solution to the problem. Peter, who was one of Christ's closest disciples, wrote in his First Letter (speaking of the death of Christ), "Christ also has died for sins once, the just [meaning Christ] for the unjust [meaning us] that he might bring us to God" [that He might bring us back into this relationship that God intended for us in creation] (1 Peter 3:18 paraphrased). Jesus Himself said, "I have come that they might have life, and that they might have it abundantly." He went on to explain that the reason He had come into human history was not only to tell us what God was like but to make it possible for us to be forgiven and cleansed and given a new life that would bring us into a vital relationship with God. The dynamic life that God wanted us to have, Christ said, was possible through personal faith and trust in Him as the One who died in our place and who rose from the dead and who today is a living Person in the twentieth century.

Someone has said of the vice-president of the United States, and it's a very solemn thought, "he's only a heartbeat away from the presidency." This same statement could be made about our relationship to God or our lack of it. If we don't have it we're only a prayer away from a dynamic relationship with the living God, our Creator. We only need to turn in faith to Jesus Christ as our Savior and Lord and express ourselves to Him in prayer, recognizing that His diagnosis of the human condition and of us as individuals is correct. We need to thank Him for having died in our place and having risen from the dead, and then we will experience the life which He offers to us as the solution to our basic inner problem.

What's wrong with the world? G. K. Chesterton put it very accurately when he said, "*I'm* wrong with the world." The way to begin solving the world's problems is to first solve our own relationship with God, for this will transform all our relationships with people around us—in our family, our community, our place of business, our campus. Only then will we begin to solve the basic problem of the world.

3

IS CHRISTIANITY RELEVANT?

One of the basic issues that is on the mind of the average non-Christian today is the question "Is Christianity relevant?" This issue is even more on the mind of the average person than the question "Is Christianity credible?" (though this is also a very prominent question on the minds of many thinking people today). Even granting that the facts of the gospel of Jesus Christ are true—that He is in fact the living Son of God, that He in fact died in our place that we might be forgiven, that He in fact rose from the dead—so what? What difference does it make?

Not long ago I was in a university discussion at Queens University in Kingston, Ontario, and after we presented the gospel for a few minutes, we opened the floor for discussion. One of the bearded graduate students took a pipe out of his mouth and looked at me in a very pitying way with the words, "Why do you Christians bother?" The full impact of what he said went far beyond his mere words, and his attitude typified what is on the minds of many people today: "Why do you Christians bother? What does your message have to do with life itself?"

Does God Understand Nuclear Energy?

Not too long ago a survey was taken among school children in a large city, and one of the questions that was asked them was, "Do you believe that God understands nuclear energy?" *Sixty-four percent of them replied no!* To their young minds God had been left in the dust of scientific progress. To them and to many other people God is mostly useful for people who have no other way to make it and need a crutch. In terms of the warp and woof of day-to-day modern living, both God and the church are totally irrelevant in the minds of many people.

One of the best ways to answer this allegation of irrelevance is to ask ourselves what characterizes modern man and to show how the Lord Jesus Christ speaks to man's needs in this twentieth-century space age. We are hearing a great deal today from the new theologians about "modern man come of age." Dietrich Bonhoeffer popularized the expression "man come of age" as a man who has outgrown his need of God, at least in the traditional Christian concept. But let's examine modern man to see if this is true, and let's see how the Lord Jesus Christ speaks to us today as the living Lord in the twentieth century.

The Lonely Crowd

What is one of the major characteristics of our time? One of the prominent ones is loneliness. Isn't it ironic that in this age of the greatest population explosion the world has ever known, when there are more bodies per square foot than there have ever been before, more people are desperately lonely than have ever been lonely before? Someone has said, "Broadway is the loneliest street in the world," and this is true even though it's one of the most crowded streets in the world. A great many things have contributed to this loneliness. For one thing, we are a rootless society, a mobile population in which people no longer live and grow up and die with the close support of their family and relatives.

We are a mobile population today, with many people caught in a "split-level trap" of lonely affluence. People are trapped within their four walls of loneliness even though they have an abundance of material things. In effect they are cut off from the society around them. Today we are a depersonalized society despite our population explosion.

Do Not Fold, Spindle, or Mutilate

I had a frightening example of depersonalization not too long ago. I kept getting a bill from one of the oil companies for 165 dollars every month because the computer had blown a transistor or suffered a monetary headache or something. I called twice and wrote three letters, but I still kept getting the 165-dollar computer card, so finally I crumpled up the card in a ball (you know, the one that says, "Do not fold, spindle, or mutilate"!) and mailed it in an envelope with a note that said, "Dear Sir: Perhaps this will get me some personal attention." And it did. I got my regular bill for 25 dollars the next month!

We have become a depersonalized society. There is suburban loneliness and there is urban loneliness. The high-rise apartments that we see all around us in so many urban neighborhoods are monuments to loneliness. Behind all those doors lies aching loneliness on the part of many people. I personally know of more than one person, both in the cities and in the suburbs, who goes to the large shopping centers simply for the opportunity of talking to somebody in the store.

At least the checker in the supermarket will speak to him as he leaves the store!

The Good Shepherd

Loneliness is one of the desperate problems of our age. Some people are lonely even within their families. What does our Lord say to the problem of loneliness? In John 10:14 He says these wonderful words: "I am the Good Shepherd; my sheep I know, and I am known of mine." I know my own sheep and they know me, says the Lord Jesus Christ. Our Lord says that when He comes into our experience as Savior and Lord, He will be our Shepherd and will never leave us or forsake us. He speaks powerfully to this question of loneliness. We need to remind ourselves of this, and we need to communicate this to a world around us that is desperately lonely.

If we are not careful, we tend to slip into the thinking of a non-Christian age. We know that no personnel manager can handle more than fifty people in any way, shape, or form, and since there are almost four billion people on the face of the earth, how can God possibly be truly concerned about me and my piddling little problems? Yet the Lord says, "I am the Good Shepherd; I know my own and my own are known of me." The very hairs of our heads are numbered, our Lord says in another place, and He also says, "Two sparrows don't fall to the ground without your heavenly Father knowing it" and "You can be sure you're worth far more than two sparrows." Christ assures us that He'll never leave us or forsake us. This is a tremendous fact to know in personal experience, and it's a fact that we can speak of with confidence to people who are lonely.

The Friend of Friends

I remember that while we were living in New York a girl came from Barnard College (associated with Columbia University) to talk to my wife. Here was a girl who had been deeply hurt, even by her own family, and now she had come to the place where she couldn't trust anybody. As my wife told her of the comforting promises of the Lord Jesus Christ, and of how He could meet this problem of loneliness in her life, she said with tears in her eyes, "You mean to say He'll never leave me, never forsake me?" Christ's assurance of His personal presence is as true as the God of the universe.

You know, a friend is defined as someone who knows the worst about us but still remains our friend. This is consummately true of our Lord. He knew He wasn't getting any prize package when He got us, but He still loves us. He knows us better than we know ourselves, and He's promised never to leave us or forsake us. I travel a great deal and am often in Podunk Junction where I don't know a soul, and it's a tremendous thing to know the experiential reality of the fact that the Lord Jesus Christ is the Good Shepherd and that I am not alone, never alone. That's a tremendous thing not only to know myself but also to enjoy and share with others.

Some years ago a doctor in Detroit became a Christian through an evangelistic crusade. He had been a profligate all his life, so about a year after his conversion some of his old cronies and friends came to him and said, "Sometimes, Doctor, when you're away from all your religious friends and their environment and all by yourself, don't you kind of wish you could get back into the old life that you used to have with is?" The doctor looked at them and said, "Yes, sometimes I do, but then I realize that I'm never alone. That's what makes the difference."

True Fellowship

Our Lord speaks powerfully to the loneliness of modern man when He says, "I am the Good Shepherd." Another dimension to this is the church of the Lord Jesus Christ, because when we come to the Savior, not only does He come into our lives and promise to be our constant companion, a Friend who sticks closer than a brother, but He also ushers us into the most wonderful fellowship in the world, the church of Jesus Christ.

I've had the privilege of traveling in some other countries, and I've had the experience (as I'm sure many of you have) of meeting someone with whom I could hardly communicate verbally but with whom there was a tremendous communication of spirit in Christ. In ten minutes we feel closer to a fellow member in the body of Christ than we do to one of our own blood relatives who doesn't know the Savior. Despite all its warts and pimples and problems, the church of the Lord Jesus Christ is still the most wonderful group of people this side of heaven.

Again, comparing the church with secular fellowhips, the church stands out even more vividly. As I said, I am often in fraternities, and it has struck me more than once that if you are a member of a secular social fraternity on a campus, you are supposed to be part of the greatest bond in life—the secret handshake and so forth. These fraternities show a close bond up to a point, but I've been in these chapter meetings more than once when a brother from, let's say, Michigan State, arrives at Columbia, Missouri, and is introduced as a member of old Psi Delta, and "Let's give Brother Jones a hand." Brother Jones is given a hand, a free meal, and a bed for the night, but then he's ignored for the rest of the evening. He's as lonely in a chapter of his own fraternity as he would be on Broadway in New

York! Sure, he's got a meal and a bed, and that's good to have, but in terms of real vital fellowship, it just isn't there.

When the church of Christ is functioning in the way it should, there is true Christian fellowship instead of superficial fraternal camaraderie. The church is the most wonderful fellowship that can be known, as you may very well have experienced yourself. Is Christianity relevant to this desperate problem of loneliness for "man come of age" in the twentieth century? Powerfully so: "I am the Good Shepherd; I know my own, and my own are known of me," says the Lord Jesus Christ.

What Does It All Mean?

Another problem of modern man that more and more secularists are writing about today is the phenomenon of meaninglessness, of lack of purpose in life. What is everything leading to? We're in this great rat race, working and striving like crazy, but what does it all lead to? What does it mean? If I had to use one category to describe students on the campuses of North America today, that category would be meaninglessness and lack of purpose. The students don't know *why* they're studying *what* they're studying apart from the fact that Mom and Dad sent them to college. Where is it all leading to? It's all so meaningless.

And, of course, this is the whole thesis of one of the major schools of philosophy today, that of existentialism, the philosophy of despair and meaninglessness. Though Shakespeare probably did not think of himself as an existentialist, he was nevertheless in that league without realizing it, for centuries ago he wrote, "Life is a tale told by an idiot, full of sound and fury, signifying nothing." That's what many people have concluded today. We popularized this despair in the philosophical language of our time. Jean-Paul Sartre, the famous French philosopher who won the Nobel Prize for his writings, produced a few years ago a play called "No Exit," which espoused essentially the same despair-oriented conclusion that Shakespeare had written of centuries earlier. Sartre also wrote a book called *Nausea,* in which the title describes life as Sartre saw it. Albert Camus, the great French novelist, speaks of the absurdity of life; meaning for him, Camus says, is accepting this meaninglessness and living on the edge of the abyss, for life itself has no real meaning.

The Light of the World

Does our Lord Jesus Christ speak to this problem? Is Christianity relevant to this problem of despair characteristic of our age? In the eighth chapter of John's Gospel, in the twelfth verse, our Lord says, "I am the light of the world; He that follows after me shall not walk in darkness, but shall have the light of life." Have you ever been in a dark room that was unfamiliar to you? Do you remember how you felt? You sort of groped your way around, and as you bumped into something your heart beat three times faster. Then something trailed across your face and you jumped three feet off the floor. You became what we might call "unzipped"—completely disoriented. For the moment you were completely insecure as you groped around trying to find the switch.

That's the way a lot of people are living life today. They're groping along the side of the wall, desperately trying to find the switch to turn the light on, because life for them has no meaning. They're trying this switch and that switch and the other switch, but they're sinking in despair because the switches are not doing for them what the searchers hoped they would. But you also know the feeling that comes to you when you find the right switch and the light goes on. Immediately you're oriented, aren't you? You know exactly where you are, and you know where everything is in relationship to everything else. Now you know how to get where you want to go. That's exactly what our Lord says He will do for us in life. "I am the Light of the world; he who follows after me shall not walk in darkness, but shall have the light of life" (John 8:12).

God's Purpose—Significance

When the Lord Jesus Christ comes into our lives as Savior and Lord, He ties our lives into God's purpose, not only for this life but for eternity. This is true significance! This is true purpose! God has a plan and a purpose for every one of us as human beings, and one of the joys of the Christian life is to allow our lives to be used in God's plan and purpose for eternity. The tremendous thing is that when we come to the Savior, the Light of the world, He promises to give us light and to show us what His will and purpose for us is. He promises to tie our lives into His own purpose for history, so that everything in our lives becomes transformed, including the routine—mowing the lawn, changing the diapers, washing the dishes, even studying physics and playing chess! *Everything* is transformed because our lives now have meaning and purpose.

Not just those so-called spiritual aspects of our lives, such as praying, reading the Bible, or witnessing, but the *totality* of our lives are given to the Savior for Him to use as He chooses. We become transformed, and we are able to do everything through His strength. Whether we eat or drink or whatever we do, we are able to do *everything* to the glory of God. This is sensational. This is the reality which we come to know when we enter into personal fellowship with the One who is the Light of the world. Is Christianity relevant to this modern age that has lost its meaning and purpose, that has lost its way? Yes, it is. The relevancy is found in Christ Himself, the only true Light of the world.

The Cold Fog

What is another problem that is characteristic of our time? One of the desperate characteristics of our time is that of emptiness, this feeling that creeps over a person like a cold fog after the party is over. It's the feeling we get when all of the external stimulations are gone, when the TV or transistor radio goes dead and we can't get it fixed until the next morning when the stores open, and we're shut up to silence, emptiness. Nothing from within. Many people today are able to exist only because of external stimulation, and they become frightened and disturbed when they're shut up to themselves, without this external stimulation on which they have depended. Psychiatrist Rollo May has coined a term to describe our age: "hollow men." That's a very apt phrase—shells, beyond the exterior of which there is nothing. Life has become completely banal.

Again, it is remarkable to me that it is the secularists, to a large extent, who are diagnosing society and individual problems in these terms. Never before have we lived in a better climate, in my opinion, to communicate the gospel, because secularists are finally beginning to realize the truth of what the Bible has said for two thousand years. And now you and I have the opportunity to share with today's crisis-ridden society the answer to life in our Lord Jesus Christ. Carl Gustav Jung, the great Swiss psychiatrist, said shortly before he died, "the central neurosis of our time is emptiness." That is the tragic characteristic of American life as well as human life throughout the world.

Better Homes and Boredom

One of the shocking things that is coming to be realized increasingly in our time is the fact that juvenile delinquency is caused, to a large extent, by boredom—sheer boredom. This is why, contrary to many analytical predictions made in years gone by, the majority of juvenile delinquents today are coming from so-called "better homes" rather than from ghettos on the other side of the tracks. Why? Because young people today are bored and empty. There is nothing within to sustain them.

The recognition of this fact is coming from remarkable quarters. Some years ago a novel was smuggled out from the Soviet Union entitled *Not by Bread Alone*. It seems that, even in that Communistic society which is dedicated to the philosophic proposition that only the material is real, many men as they begin to think and reflect are coming to realize that this philosophy is not true, that there must be something beyond the material to sustain the spirit of man.

The Bread and Water of Life

What does our Lord say to this problem of emptiness which is so characteristic of our time? In John 6:35 our Lord says, "I am the Bread of life; he who comes to me shall never hunger, and he who believes on me shall never thirst." What does this mean? It means that, as we come into personal relationship with the Lord Jesus Christ and remain in this vital relationship day by day, He sustains us from within. Our Lord Himself said to the disciples when they were concerned as to whether He had anything to eat after His conversation with the woman at the well, "I have meat to eat that you know not of . . . to do the will of him who sent me" (John 4:32, 34).

In a measure we can share in that spiritual meat as we come to know Him who is the Bread and Water of life. As we seek to do His will, we have meat to eat that others do not know about; we are sustained inwardly by the Holy Spirit, by the One who is the Bread and Water of life. We are sustained in that dimension of life that can never be satisfied by cramming with material things.

4

THE POWER OF CHRIST

We had a very vivid illustration of the principle of Christ versus materialism in Fort Lauderdale several years ago. As you may know, every Easter we set up informal evangelistic bull sessions with students on the beach, and the students are astounded that anybody would come and talk seriously with them about the issues of life (and they're very interested, too, I might add). One evening when we went back to the hotel, the owner of the hotel gave his personal testimony. Mr. Charles Pitts of Toronto stood up and told these students that his personal ambition in life had been to make a million dollars by the time he was 40 years old. He said, "By the time I was 35 years old I had made my first million, and by the time I was 40 I had made six million." This wasn't hard to believe as we looked around at this plush hotel of which Mr. Pitts was the owner!

Then he went on to say that he had felt the answer to life was to get everything you could desire, and "when I didn't have it, I thought that would give me satisfaction, but as I increasingly acquired more and more things, I found that I was not satisfied and it did not satisfy the emptiness of my life." His wife became restless and dissatisfied, so he bought her homes in three or four places around the world, trying desperately to satiate her longing for material things. But this didn't seem to work either.

Any Port in a Storm?

Then Mr. Pitts told the students how, after a period of time, his wife began to read the Bible and get comfort from it. He thought this was kind of a nutty thing to do, but if it calmed her, well, any port would do in a storm, so he bought her a couple of Bibles for her to read. Soon she seemed to undergo a whole change of outlook toward life. She talked about knowing Christ personally, though to him this was so much gobbledygook. Mr. Pitts didn't understand all this religious stuff—he thought it was nonsense and certainly not for him. Perhaps it was okay for an emotional woman who was disturbed, but certainly not for a hardheaded businessman.

But then Mr. Pitts related how he increasingly realized that his life was not giving him all that he wanted. At the request of his wife he went very reluctantly to an evangelistic meeting in 1959 while his planes were warming up at the airport that very evening to fly west for his annual hunting trip. He told how God the Holy Spirit got hold of him that night, and how he came to the Savior. Mr. Pitts closed his testimony with the words, "I found what I had been looking for all my life; I can tell you who are at the bottom rung of the ladder that when you get to the top of the ladder, you don't find what you are looking for unless you have got Jesus Christ to satisfy that emptiness which is inherent in human nature separated from God our Maker."

This testimony had a profound impact on those students because they realized that they were at the bottom rung of the ladder. To hear from someone who had obviously made it that getting further up the ladder doesn't in itself satisfy these inner longings made a deep impact.

Happiness over the Horizon?

If we're not married, we think, "Well, things aren't too good now, but when we get married, that will solve it." If we're not making too much money now, we think, "Well, when we get enough income coming in, that will do it." Then we get the first job and we think, "Well, it must come after the next promotion." And so forth and so on, with the first car and the second, and always it's the next thing over the horizon, the next thing over the hill, to satisfy this emptiness.

No, our Lord says, "I am the Bread of life; he who eats of me shall never hunger, and he who drinks of me shall never thirst." The tremendous thing that happens when we come into personal relationship with the Lord Jesus Christ, the thing which we can communicate with confidence and power to our friends, is that we receive a life and a deep-seated joy that enable us to transcend all our circumstances.

Transcending Circumstances

Most people apart from Christ are tied to circumstances. When they're up, they're up, and when they're down, they're down. But if we really know Christ and are in vital fellowship with Him, we are able to transcend circumstances, whatever they may be. This reality is what enabled Paul to say, "I have learned in whatever state I am, therewith to be content." He didn't appreciate prisons and scorpions and snakes and rats any more than you or I do, but he had something that went far beyond that to sustain him. It was the reality of Christ that sent the early Christians singing to the den of lions. It wasn't the circumstances, it was knowing the One who is the Bread and Water of life.

We are not immune to circumstances; the tragedies and sufferings of life have their impact on us, but we have Someone in those circumstances who enables us to transcend them. We have an inner contentment, an inner peace, that goes far beyond the temporary waves on the surface as we come to know the One who is the Bread and Water of life. "I am the bread of life; he who eats of me shall never hunger, and he who drinks of me shall never thirst." Let me ask those of you who know Christ personally, are you enjoying to the full all that you have in the Lord Jesus Christ? It's only as you enjoy Him in experiential reality that you are able to speak with conviction and power to those around who ask the question, "Are Jesus Christ and the gospel relevant to our times today?"

Moral Power Failure

Another problem that we face in our society today is what I call a moral power failure. We are finding a breakdown in ethical morality at every level of our society: in government, in industry, in business, and most certainly on the campuses. The shocking campus immorality is one of the clear indications to me that, as valuable as education is, it doesn't solve the basic problem of human nature. If the basic problem of human nature were ignorance, then surely the universities, which presumably have more information than any other segment of society, would be the most moral segment of society. Unfortunately, this is not the case. Knowledge is not the same thing as virtue. *Knowing* what is right to do and *doing* it are two very different things.

I talk to many people, students and others, who *know* what is right but find themselves *doing*, sometimes continuously, things that they would never have dreamed possible of themselves. They hate themselves for it afterwards, but they find themselves almost helplessly drawn to the same sins again. Secular novelists and playwrights are describing these things to us. You don't have to go to productions to know what's going on. If you read reviews in *Time* magazine, for example, you know what's going on.

More than Good Advice

Knowing what to do and doing it are not the same thing. People who are in this situation need more than just good advice. If all the Lord did when He came into human history was just to give us a Sermon on the Mount, as wonderful and great as that Sermon was, all He would have done was increase our frustration. We've had some kind of golden rule from the earliest dawn of history, from the time of Confucius on down. But our Lord did far more than this; He said, "I am the life" and "I am come that they might have life, and that they might have it more abundantly" (John 14:6; 10:10).

I have the privilege of being on the faculty of Trinity Evangelical Divinity School in Deerfield, Illinois, and one of the courses I teach is the history of religion and the Christian approach to non-Christian religions. I have been impressed again and again, as I have restudied this material, with the uniqueness of the Lord Jesus Christ. Every other religious leader of the world says essentially, "This is the way; if you take this way and succeed, you will make it at the end." But the problem is, of course, that nobody can make it.

But the Lord is the reverse. He doesn't give a set of swimming instructions to a drowning man. He says, "I am the way. You come to me and I will give you my life." The reason the Christian is able to live a life that is supernatural is because the life that he has in the Lord Jesus Christ is supernatural. How is it possible to love somebody who is inherently unlovely? It's not possible by pumping ourselves up and saying, "I ought to love him. I ought to love him. I am going to think positively and come to this." No. It is because the Lord Jesus Christ comes into our lives as the One who is the life. As we by faith lay hold of Him, He releases this life in us so that we are able to live in the reality and the power which He offers us.

Not a Path, But a Person

Someone has suggested, and I think very aptly, that the Christian life is not so much a *path* as it is a *Person*. Christ is our life, and we look to Him day by day in faith. In all those circumstances of life in which we realize that we don't have the power to do what we know we should do, we find our Lord coming to us and releasing His power into our lives. What the world needs today, and what you and I need to proclaim, is that power which is strong enough to change human nature itself.

Everybody knows that war is wrong, but knowledge doesn't change war or stop war. Knowledge does not produce virtue. We need a power which is strong enough to make a liar tell the truth, to make a profligate pure, to make a thief honest. We need a power that can break the chain of drug addiction, that can break the prison of alcoholism, that can make all of us holy people in God's sight.

This power is Jesus Christ Himself. "I am the life," He says—not His teaching, which is important, but "*I personally* am the life." The dynamic of Christianity is the fact that the Lord Jesus Christ is a living Person today who can invade the life of any person who invites Him to come in. You and I are able to live in the reality of this relationship today because Christ is risen. He is not just a good idea; He is a personality. "I am come," He says, "that they might have life more abundantly." Does our Lord speak to the problem of moral power failure? Powerfully. He is the One, the only One, who can help us when we cannot help ourselves.

The Problem of Guilt

What's another problem? The problem of guilt. It's very characteristic of our society today. Again, secularists are commenting on this, and increasingly they are coming to realize that there is a distinction, a vast distinction, between guilt and a guilt complex. A guilt complex is some vague fear of having lost a button when I was three years old and still feeling very guilty about it. There is no rational basis for this feeling of guilt. However, as Dr. O. Hobart Mowrer of the University of Illinois has pointed out in his book *The Crisis in Psychiatry and Religion,* guilt is an absolutely normative part of human personality. If you stab your mother to death and feel no guilt about it, there is something tragically abnormal about you. There is a normative aspect of guilt in human personality which is quite distinct from guilt complexes. (These are real, too, but have no rational basis for existing.)

At Queens University in Kingston a man got into our discussion and told how, a year before, he had come to know the Lord Jesus Christ through Dr. Fred Smith of the University of

Minnesota. The man said in this discussion, "My life was so racked up that I didn't know which way to turn. I was so corrupt from within that I needed a bath from the inside out. When I came to know Christ," he added, "I got that bath, I just can't describe the difference to you. For 24 hours after this happened to me I just sat thinking about its implication, it was so profound in its impact on me."

Does our Lord speak to our gnawing guilt? He says in John 10:9, "I am the door; by me if any man enters in, he shall be saved, and shall go in and out and find pasture." Paul alludes to this same forgiveness in 2 Corinthians 5:21—"He [God] has made him [Jesus Christ] to be sin for us, who knew no sin, that we might be made the righteousness of God in him." When we come to the Savior as the Door to heaven we are saved; we experience forgiveness and cleansing from within. This is a tremendous reality to a world that knows it has sin and desperately wants forgiveness and cleansing.

Restlessness

Another problem that we have today is restlessness. The phenomenal sale of books on peace of mind and soul, and variations on that theme, indicates that whatever these authors are saying, they have touched a chord that is on the minds of many people today. If you speak on the subject of inner peace today, you inevitably attract a crowd. Most people have no inner peace. A doctor friend of mine on the West Coast took an informal poll over a period of three years. He asked his patients, "If you had one desire that you knew would be granted without any question, what would you ask?" Eighty-seven percent of the respondents said they would ask for peace of mind and soul!

A few weeks ago we held a discussion in one of our Midwestern suburbs with a number of scientists from around the world. A presentation of the gospel was made, and we were discussing Christianity afterward. One very brilliant man, a Ph.D., said, "I don't see this Christianity business. I've got everything you Christians have. I've got a lovely home, I love my wife, I'm kind to my neighbor, and I pay my bills." But then he paused for a moment and added, "The only thing is, I can't sleep at night." How tragic!

My Peace I give unto You

We began to discuss how the Lord Jesus Christ could meet this scientist's problem of inner turmoil, and I believe he's now on the way to the Kingdom. Our Lord says in John 14:27, "Peace I leave with you; my peace I give unto you. Not as the world gives do I give unto you. Let not your heart be troubled, neither let it be afraid." In Matthew 11:28 He says, "Come unto me, all you who labor and are heavily laden, and I will give you rest." Rest and peace are wonderful words, aren't they? They're the kind of words you want to suck on, so to speak, to use a candy illustration. They are so comforting. This comfort we can have through our Lord Jesus Christ, who speaks with such powerful relevance to the problem of inner turmoil today.

The Fear of Death

Anxiety is another problem in our society today, and secularists are recognizing this problem. Fear of the future and fear of death grip many of us. They don't grip us when we're sitting in a nice warm room with friends, but when we're facing surgery, it's a horse of another color. Sooner or later death becomes a very real thing to us. Does our Lord speak to this fear of death? In John 11:25, 26 He says, "I am the resurrection and the life; he who believes in me, though he were dead, yet shall he live, and whoever lives and believes in me shall never die." One of our Lord's tremendous relevancies to life today is that *He* is the resurrection and the life; *He* delivers us from fear of the future. We know our lives are in His hand, that nothing happens by accident, because death for us is merely an ushering into the presence of God for all eternity.

I used to wonder whether Christ could really

60

give peace at a time of death. One of the by-products of my heart surgery in 1954 was that I proved experientially in my own life that the peace of Christ is real. I had always *said* it was real, but it's quite another thing to face the fact of death for yourself! I'll never forget the tremendous peace that came into my heart and soul as I was wheeled into that operating room. I knew this peace came not from within but from without. I knew I would probably survive the surgery, but I also knew that there was a distinct possibility I wouldn't make it. When you're fooling around with the human heart, the operation can be a technical success and the patient still die because one of 73 other things went wrong! It was a tremendous thing for me to experience the reality of the Lord Jesus Christ as the resurrection and the life. This our Lord speaks to with powerful relevance in our time.

I Am the Truth

There are other things which we could mention. Our Lord says, "I am the truth." It's phenomenal how quickly intellectual confusion begins to evaporate when we come to the One who is *the* truth. Some modern intellectuals are finding this today—certainly many students are. Is Christianity relevant? Simply review the problems of life today, of modern man come of age, and of the problems of the people whom you know, and then ask yourself how the Lord Jesus speaks to this. Enter into the experiential reality of this by faith yourself, and then communicate it to others. Both you and your hearers will find that we have the most relevant and powerful message that the world could possibly hear.

5

IS CHRISTIANITY CREDIBLE?

"Is Christianity credible?" This question is feared by both friends and enemies of the Christian faith. Friends of the Christian faith fear it because, if the truth were known, many Christians wonder if Christianity would really hold water if it were exposed to the full light of truth and investigation. They have faith, and they're hanging onto it and are going to believe it, but they sometimes wonder if the thing would really stand on its own feet if it were fully and completely investigated. They're not too sure but that the little Sunday school boy was correct when he defined faith by saying, "Well, faith is believing something you know isn't really true." Some Christians think in their heart of hearts that perhaps this is really the essence of the matter.

On the other hand, the question "Is Christianity credible?" is also feared by enemies of the Christian faith, since they recognize that the question carries a tremendous implication for life. If it were to turn out that Christianity is in fact credible and true, this would have enormous implications for their personal life and relationship to Jesus Christ. So this question makes many enemies of the Christian faith feel edgy too.

An Element Called Faith

In the minds of many people, the problem of the credibility of Christianity has to do with the fact that Christianity requires an element of faith. The word "faith" makes a lot of people nervous, particularly a lot of thinking people, and the reason is that "faith" in our society today is a very mushy, oozy, foggy word. It really has very little content. An airplane comes in safely after having developed engine trouble and the passengers ask the pilot, "How did you do it?" He says, "Well, we came in by faith," and everybody gets a warm, glowy feeling inside. They're not quite sure what he means, but faith is so wonderful, and they feel great. Or you're about to flunk out of school and somebody slaps you on the back and says, "Well, that's all right, just have faith." You know, cheer up and try to be happy. The word "faith" as used this way really doesn't mean a thing, but it sounds wonderful and everybody gets so happy when they use the word this way. But the more thoughtful people recognize that this kind of faith is a rather vague concept, so they begin to wonder whether, in the final analysis, faith is not essentially superstition.

Some people say to those who have a personal relationship with Jesus Christ, "I just wish I had your faith—it's wonderful. I just wish I had it, but I just can't believe." Now some people have real problems in believing. But what most people mean, when they say they can't believe, is "The problem is that I've just got a little bit too much upstairs, and I can't be quite that naive. It must be wonderful to be that simple-minded, and I wish I could be, but I can't quite bring myself to do it."

The Elephant-Chaser
of Grant Park

There are many people who really feel that there is no more cause-and-effect relationship between faith and reality than with the story of the elephant-chaser in Grant Park. He sat in the park reading a paperback book, and as he read each page he ripped it out of the book, tore it up in little pieces, and scattered the pieces all around the bench. Interesting, to say the least! He did this with page after page of the book.

Pretty soon a policeman observed the man doing this, and after a couple of minutes the policeman came up to him and said, "Sir, apart from the fact that you're littering the ground, I wonder if you would mind telling me why, after you read each page, you tear it out of the book and scatter it on the ground?" The fellow brightened and said, "Sure, it's to keep the elephants away." The policeman replied, "To keep the elephants away? I don't see any elephants." The fellow responded, "Yeah, pretty effective, isn't it?"

That's exactly the kind of nonexistent cause-and-effect relationship that many people identify with faith and reality. They think it's a sort of "keeping-the-elephants-away" concept, and so they don't see how a thinking person could become involved in a vital personal faith in Jesus Christ.

Faith and Its Object

Now when we discuss this question of faith, there are three observations that we must keep in mind before we can discuss the question intelligently. The first observation is that *faith is no more valid than the object in which it is placed*, whether that object is a person or a thing. If the object of our faith is valid, we have valid faith. If the object of our faith is invalid, we have nothing more than superstition.

Let's think for a moment of a witch doctor in

some primitive culture in the world. He prepares a brew that he gives to a desperately anxious father whose little daughter is seriously ill with a high fever. The father takes the potion to his daughter because he has intense faith and belief. He is very sincere, but his sincerity doesn't save the life of his daughter if the witch doctor's potion happens to be poisonous. In this case the father's faith amounts to nothing more than superstition, since the object of his faith is invalid. The validity of faith is determined by its *object* and not by its *intensity*.

Don't Believe Everything

This leads us to a second observation: believing something false doesn't make it true, and failing to believe something true doesn't make it false. Merely believing something, however wonderful the thing is, doesn't create truth, and failing to believe something, no matter how distasteful it is, doesn't erase its factuality.

To illustrate the point that believing something doesn't make it true, I heard about a little old lady who rented a room to what she thought was a very nice, brightly scrubbed, intelligent college student in a college town. She continued to think he was a lovely boy with a fine, upstanding character until she came home one day and found the whole place cleaned out— nothing but the curtain rods left. She mournfully told the police when they came around to investigate, "Oh, my, but he was such a nice boy; he even had YMCA on his towel." Well, believing something doesn't create truth! She believed implicitly in the young man, but that didn't save her possessions!

The Starving Millionaire

On the other hand, failing to believe something doesn't erase truth. Several years ago a poverty-stricken recluse in Texas (you know, one of those people with cats running around and the place stuffed with newspapers) was informed that he had inherited a million dollars from a relative in England whom he didn't even realize existed. It was a fact—the recluse was heir to a million dollars. He could have taken advantage of that fact, living high on the hog with three cars and eighteen suits. But, tragically, he didn't believe that fact and died a starving old man. His failure to believe that he was heir to a million dollars didn't change the fact. He was still heir to the million dollars. But what his unbelief did was to totally rob him of the enjoyment of his wealth.

This is the point: faith enables us to enter into the reality of that which is already true, but it doesn't create truth out of something which is not objectively true already. Nor does lack of faith erase truth; what's true is true, and our opinion of the truth doesn't change the fact of truth one bit. There's nothing spooky about the word "faith"; it simply means confident trust in something that is true.

Everyone Uses Faith

The third observation is this: every one of us exercises faith every day we live. There's a strange notion going around in some circles that faith is something reserved for a small group of peculiar people—you know, you either have it or you don't; it's wonderful if you have it but if you don't have it, well, that's just too bad. But the fact is that faith is *not* something reserved for a particular type of emotionally constructed person; faith is something that *every one of us exercises every day we live*.

Some of you may have had lunch in a restaurant at noon today. If so, you ate food that you didn't see prepared (and maybe if you had seen it prepared, you wouldn't have eaten it!). I submit to you that you ate that food in blind faith, and just how blind you may never know unless you go behind the scenes. I worked for a restaurant one summer, so I know whereof I speak!

The point is that all of us exercise faith. Now we all try to exercise *reasonable* faith (people weren't dropping like flies from ptomaine poisoning in your favorite restaurant, we assume), but you did nevertheless exercise faith when you ate there. The student who enrolls in a college exercises faith in that college; he assumes that after completing a certain series of course requirements he will be awarded a degree. If he didn't believe that, he would transfer to the most odious rival possible. If he thought that this year the institution would suddenly say, "Well, we don't want to be conformists, so this year we're not going to award any degrees," he would change schools immediately. People exercise *faith* in the college of their choice!

Science and Faith

Even the scientific method itself, which we all recognize to be one of the most objective mechanisms by which we come to the experience of reality, ultimately rests upon faith. Three unproven axioms must be accepted by faith before we can proceed with the scientific method: first, the continuity of yesterday, today, and tomorrow; second, the reliability of our sense perceptions; and third, the orderliness of the universe. We accept these by faith in order to make scientific progress. If we didn't believe these assumptions there would be no basis at all for the scientific method. Even the most objective method of determining reality has within it an element of faith. Faith is really nothing to be afraid of!

The real question is not whether one person

has faith and another person doesn't (since all of us have faith); the real question is whether the object of our faith is worth trusting. When we're discussing the question "Is Christianity credible?", we recognize that the object of one's Christian faith is Jesus Christ, so the $64,000 question we must ask ourselves is, "Is Jesus Christ a valid object for my faith? Is He a trustworthy Person? Is He someone to whom I can commit myself with confidence?" This is the question we must ask ourselves, and in order to answer it we must examine two basic lines of evidence: external evidence and internal evidence. We'll look at the external evidence first and discuss the internal aspects later in this book.

The Facts of the Gospels

The external evidence about Christ is totally outside our own personal experience because it deals with the solid facts of history. There is a large body of historical facts about Jesus Christ, and if we're honest in our approach we must face up to them forthrightly. One of the groups of data that we are confronted with are the four Gospels in the New Testament: Matthew, Mark, Luke, and John.

Regardless of our point of view with reference to the inspiration of these particular documents, we must recognize that they are historical documents which have been well validated. Sir William Ramsay, the famous nineteenth-century archeologist from Great Britain, stated that Luke was one of the most accurate historians of his time (Luke, of course, being a medical physician). These four Gospel accounts are documentary biographies of Jesus Christ that present to us a whole body of information about this unique person, Jesus of Nazareth. They are rather remarkable documents when we come to grips with them, for one of the things that even a superficial reading of the four Gospels tells us with striking force is that *Jesus Christ literally claimed to be God in human form.*

I think sometimes the electricity of this claim escapes us in the twentieth century.

If I were to stand here and say, "Ladies and gentlemen, do you want to know what God is like? Take a look," it would be frighteningly bad, actually blasphemous. You would immediately (if you really thought I was serious) excuse yourself to get the men with the white coats before I started getting violent or something!

Jesus Christ Is God

But Jesus Christ was in dead earnest when he identified Himself as the living God. There's no mistaking His claim to deity, because as we know from reading the four Gospels this was the very claim that led to Christ's ultimate execution and crucifixion. Christ was killed because He claimed to be God. His enemies said, "We have a law, and by this law this man ought to die." This law was the law against blasphemy—a mere man making himself into God—and so Jesus Christ was executed. In terms that most of us are probably familiar with, Christ made His claim very explicit, and His hearers got the message. There was no doubt in their minds; there was no obscurity about the whole thing; Christ was claiming deity for Himself.

There are a number of instances of this claim in the New Testament, and one particularly important one occurs in the tenth chapter of the Gospel of John. Jesus said to the Jews (verse 30), "I and my Father are one," and it says that they took up stones to stone him (verse 31). Then Jesus replied, "I have shown you many good works from my Father; for which of these works do you stone me?" (verse 32). But the Jews answered, "We stone you for no good work, but for blasphemy, because you, being a man, make yourself to be God" (verse 33).

A little later, after Christ had been speaking to His disciples, Philip said to Him, "Lord, show us the Father, and it will be enough for us" (John 14:8). Jesus turned to Philip and in very remarkable words said to him, "Philip, have I been with you so long and you still do not know who I am? He who has seen me has seen the

73

Father" (John 14:9). Staggering words in their implication! A claim that must be faced sooner or later by all of us.

6

THE TRUTH OF CHRIST

Somehow we must explain the staggering claims of Jesus Christ, and I submit to you that there are only four possible explanations of His claims to deity. One possibility is that Christ was a liar— that He knew He was not God but deliberately deceived people in an attempt to give weight to His particular brand of religious teaching. To postulate that Christ was a liar is a shocking thing right on the surface, and not many people hold to this point of view, since even people who deny that Jesus Christ was God immediately hasten to assure us that He was at least a great moral philosopher and teacher. However, these people don't realize the stark inconsistency of this position. If Christ was wrong on the most crucial point of His teaching, He could hardly be considered a great teacher of any kind. The fact is that it's simply incredible that the propounder of the most widely acclaimed ethical system in the world could have been a deliberate liar.

Megalomania?

The second possibility is that Christ was a lunatic. Again, that's a bald statement, but we do need to get right down to the brass tacks of this issue. Some people would say that Christ was sincere but had lost contact with reality—sort of like people today who think they're Napoleon or George Washington or, in fact, Jesus Christ. And of course our mental institutions have lots of people who suffer from this particular mental disturbance.

But we know today what the symptoms of paranoia and megalomania are, and as we compare the life of Jesus Christ with what we know these clinical symptoms to be, we find no comparison at all. On the contrary, Jesus Christ manifested symptoms and characteristics of sublime sanity and dignity. He was tremendouly poised in the midst of enormous pressure—for example, at the time of His death. When Christ's very life was at stake, He was the quintessence of poise and composure, so much so that even His enemies were astonished. Pontius Pilate, the hardened Roman governor who held Christ's earthly life in his hands, couldn't understand the composure of this Man at this particular point of crisis.

A Legend?

The third possibility is that the whole thing is a legend, that Christ really never said these things in the first place. What actually happened, according to this theory, is that Christ's enthusiastic followers in the third and fourth centuries got carried away with themselves and put words in Christ's mouth that He would be shocked to hear and would immediately disown if He were back on earth today. According to this theory, the whole story of Christ is essentially a legend developed over a period of time, since people tend to legendize everybody and everything significant.

This point of view was held very widely in many quarters about fifty years ago, but the problem with this thesis is that the most recent archeological discoveries (of which there have been an enormous wealth, as you probably know) have demonstrated conclusively that the Gospels and much of the rest of the New Testament were written not in the third and fourth centuries, as had previously been supposed, but rather within the lifetimes of the very contemporaries of Jesus Christ. According to the late William F. Albright, one of the world's leading archeologists, some of Paul's letters could easily have been written as early as 50 A.D., and there is no reason to believe that any book in the New Testament was written later than 70 A.D.

No Time Lag

We now know that the documents about Christ were written during the lifetimes of the contemporaries of Christ Himself, and so the time lag necessary for this elaborate kind of legend to develop just wasn't there. For a legend to have gained this kind of credence and acceptance without ever having taken place would be as absolutely fantastic as somebody in our time writing a book about the late President Franklin Delano Roosevelt and saying that he claimed to be God, claimed to forgive people's sins, claimed that he was going to rise from the dead, and in fact did rise from the dead.

I've heard President Roosevelt accused of a lot of things, but I've never heard him accused of these kinds of claims. The whole thing would be so wild that it would never get off the ground, since there are just too many people around who knew Roosevelt and knew that he never made any such claims. We must never delude ourselves into thinking that the people who lived during New Testament times were all sort of naive, sheepish people who were very uncritical and believed everything they heard. I think we sometimes fail to realize that quite a few people were bitterly antagonistic toward Jesus Christ and Christianity at that time, even to the point of murder (just as in our time). Some people of the first century would have given anything to see Christianity strangled in its cradle, but the truth of Christ prevailed against even its most bitter opposition.

The Four Possibilities

Jesus Christ, then, in terms of His claim to deity, was either a liar, a legend, a lunatic, or the truth. These are the only four possibilities. As I've suggested numbers of times in university audiences, if we say we don't believe that Jesus Christ is the truth, we are automatically claiming, whether we realize it or not, that Christ was a liar, a lunatic, or a legend. If we make such a claim we need to ask ourselves, "What evidence can we produce to confirm this particular point of view, evidence which would persuade a truly thoughtful person?"

I often have an eager student come roaring up to me suggesting possibility number five, but invariably this "fifth possibility" is just a slight variation on one of the other four possibilities. There are only four possibilities, and if we say that Christ is not the truth, we are automatically affirming one of the other three positions. The claim of Jesus Christ is quite clear: it is a piece of history we must grapple with and explain in one way or another.

The Credentials of Christ

Since talk is cheap, the heart of the issue about Christ's claim to deity is *the credentials He presents* in order to substantiate His claim to deity. If *I* were to make this claim to deity I'm sure it wouldn't take you very long to disprove my claim, and I suspect that if *you* were to make the claim it wouldn't take me very long to disprove yours either! But the astounding thing is that when we come to the claim of Jesus Christ, we find that it is not easy at all to disprove His claim to deity, since He provided the credentials to substantiate His claim and to demonstrate that He spoke the truth

For one thing, Christ lived a life of such utter moral perfection that even His enemies were unable to challenge Him on this point. Most of us would hesitate to expose ourselves completely to even our closest friends, to challenge them to find anything wrong with us. But Jesus Christ said to His enemies, "Which of you can convict me of sin?" And none of them could. If you read through the four Gospels you'll find that all of Christ's enemies, including Pilate, the Roman governor, said in effect, "We agree. This man has never done anything wrong. He lived a life of absolute moral perfection."

The Authority of God

Christ did things that demonstrated that He had the authority of God over the physical elements of the universe—He healed people, He raised people from the dead, He controlled the winds and the waves, and he did many other supernatural things. But the supreme test of Christ was His prediction made five times over during the course of His earthly life that He was going to die but rise from the dead three days later. Now that's a rather acid test, I think you would have to agree.

I think the electricity of this, the jarringness of it, doesn't get to us in the twentieth century, since it was one of those things that happened long ago and far away. But suppose I were to say to you in person, "I don't feel too well, and as a matter of fact I think I'm going to pass out and die, to be quite honest about the whole thing. But don't worry about getting anybody for that speaking engagement I'm going to have Sunday, because I'll tell you what's going to happen—I'm coming back from the dead on Sunday morning." Well, I think you might excuse yourself to go out and get the people with the white coats before I should break loose completely!

The Resurrection of Christ

But this is exactly what Jesus Christ predicted. Five times He predicted that He would die but rise again from the dead. And the record that we have is that this is precisely what happened— that Jesus Christ rose bodily from the dead. Christ's empty tomb is the universal symbol of Christianity, and inspires the Easter Sunday that we celebrate every year. This single fact of Christ's resurrection is what revolutionized that frightened band of Christian disciples who were so chicken that one of them once denied that he ever knew Christ!

This is what changed the disciples into roaring lions, so that fifty days later Peter, the Christ-denier, stood up and preached to two thousand people right in Jerusalem, the very place that he had denied Christ. Peter had the newfound courage to say, "This same Jesus, whom you crucified, God has raised from the dead, whereby we have become eyewitnesses."

Now if the resurrection didn't happen and the record of it is a fable, we've simply got to explain it away in one way or another, and this is a remarkably difficult thing to do. The resurrection has well been called the best-attested fact of ancient history. Let me suggest to you one alternative theory that has been advanced and which, on the surface, seems rather plausible in explaining away the resurrection. Let me show why this theory is inadequate and why, in fact, the only thing that adequately explains the history of the first century as we know it is the fact of the resurrection of Christ from the dead.

The Hallucination Theory

I was in college when I first heard about the hallucination theory, and for the moment it sounded very plausible to me—in fact, I didn't know why I hadn't thought of it myself. The hallucination theory says that Christ's followers just sort of talked themselves into believing Christ's resurrection. You know, they thought about it and thought about it and pretty soon they persuaded themselves that the whole thing had happened. Then they began to perusade other people, and pretty soon the whole thing grew into a widely accepted view. This theory sounds rather plausible until we recognize that to have a hallucination we must so intensely want to believe something that we ruminate on it, think about it, project it, and attach a reality out there, and finally we begin to move in that direction. But this first and absolute requirement, the intense desire to believe the resurrection, was strikingly absent from the record of the life of the disciples.

The Doubting Disciples

Take Mary, for instance. We have the record in each of the four Gospels, and in greatest detail in the twentieth chapter of John's Gospel, that on Easter Sunday morning she came to the tomb. What did she have in her hands? Spices for entombment. Why did she have these spices? Not because she was expecting to see Jesus Christ rise from the dead, but because she wanted to anoint the dead body. So much was she *not* expecting to see Christ alive from the dead that, when He spoke to her, she failed to recognize Him and mistook Him for the gardener with the words, "Sir, where have they lain him?" She didn't get the message, didn't recognize Christ, until He addressed her by name.

When the women who had been at the tomb heard the message of resurrection from the angels, they ran to tell the eleven disciples, but the men accused the women of dreaming up fairy tales (Luke 24:1-11). Later, when Christ appeared to the disciples in Jerusalem, they were so surprised that they thought they were seeing a ghost, and Jesus had to invite them to actually reach out and touch Him (Luke 24:36-40). This hardly lends weight to the hallucination theory!

Doubting Thomas

The classic example of unbelief was, of course, "doubting Thomas," whom we still refer to in this way even in the twentieth century. We have the record of his experience in the twentieth chapter of John's Gospel. Because he had not been with the disciples the first time Christ appeared, Thomas said "Friends, Romans, countrymen, I'm an empiricist—I don't believe unless I can see. I'm from Missouri, I want to be shown. Unless I can put my finger in His hand and my hand in His side, I will not believe." Thomas wasn't about to have a hallucination! Remember how Christ later on met with Thomas again, and as "doubting Thomas" came into a personal confrontation with Christ he declared the tremendous words, "My Lord and my God!" On the basis of this encounter with Christ, Thomas became convinced against his will, so to speak, that Jesus Christ had risen from the dead. The actual, literal resurrection of Christ is truly the only event that adequately explains the history of the first century.

The Modern-Day Thomas

There's a modern-day Thomas in which some of you might be interested, a British lawyer by the name of Frank Morison. In the early 1930's Morison was convinced that Christianity was nothing but a tissue of fabric and fable and superstition. He correctly realized that the foundation stone of Christianity was the resurrection of Christ, and he felt that if he could show conclusively that the resurrection was a fraud and a figment of the first-century imagination, he would once-and-for-all rid the world of Christianity, thereby doing it a great favor. Morison was a lawyer, and he felt that he had the critical apparatus to rigidly evaluate evidence, throwing out anything that didn't meet the criteria that are necessary for evidence to be introduced into a court of law. So he set out to prove that the resurrection never happened.

However, when Morison's book was finally published, the first chapter had a curious title: "The Book that Refused to Be Written." In this chapter Morison described how he became persuaded against his will that the resurrection had indeed taken place. By examining the evidence, Morison had to acknowledge that the resurrection of Jesus Christ had indeed taken place and was one of the greatest facts of world history. Morison's book is titled *Who Moved the Stone?* and is published by Zondervan Publishing House.

Knowing Christ Personally

The second avenue of evidence about the reality of Christ's claim to deity has to do with contemporary, personal, experiential knowledge of Christ—the *personal* verification of the objective facts of history. If Jesus Christ is who He claims to be, then He can and will do in our lives today all the things He promises to do. The real dynamic of Christianity is that Jesus Christ is alive today, having risen from the dead. He is no longer in that tomb, but is a living Personality with whom we can communicate and who will respond to us. We can know Him today in the twentieth century, in our own personal experience.

We can conduct an experiment to validate the hypothesis that Jesus Christ is, as He claimed, the Son of God and the Savior of the world. The experimental laboratory in this instance is the laboratory of human life. If we meet Jesus Christ on His conditions, that is, on the basis of His substitutionary death and resurrection, we can in our own experience verify the hypothesis that Christ is who He claimed to be. We will find Christ doing in our lives those things He says He will do, giving us inner peace and directing our lives into God's purpose for history.

Christ promises to give us new moral power and to free us of the slavery to our sinful selves to which all of us have succumbed. He promises to be to us spiritual bread and food, so that our spiritual hunger and thirst can be quenched with that reality that comes only from knowing the true and living God. Christ promises to forgive our sins and to cleanse us from guilt, to give us forgiveness which we cannot buy or work out in any other way. And there are many other things that Jesus Christ says He can and will do in the life of a person who comes into personal relationship with Him.

Modern Conversion Data

The interesting thing is that we have actual

clinical data in the twentieth century by which we can come to grips with this issue. There are many people in our time from every conceivable background who have had their lives transformed by Jesus Christ. It is not only (as some people think) those who have been raised in Christian homes who become Christians. Many people who have had very little contact with Christianity have discovered Him to be the answer to the riddle of life and have had their views transformed by Him. Their experience cannot in any way be explained on a Pavlovian dog basis. (As you recall, Pavlov fed the dogs and rang a bell at the same time, and the dogs learned to salivate. Eventually he rang the bell and didn't feed them and they still salivated, with the reaction occurring from just the psychological association.) There are those who suggest that this is the way all Christian experience is—you condition people in a Christian environment, push the button at the right time, the bell rings, and they become Christians.

No Pavlovian Dogs

But the explanation is not quite that simple, since many people become Christians despite no religious background at all. One thing all of these people bear testimony to is the life-changing experience they undergo when they encounter Jesus Christ as a living Person. Whether you talk to a person who had no contact with Jesus Christ before becoming a Christian, or to a person who was raised in a Christian environment, both acknowledge that Jesus Christ became personal to them through that vital step of personal commitment. Both of them bear testimony to the fact that the transformation that took place in their lives happened through a personal encounter with Jesus Christ.

I can think of a number of students (as well as nonstudents) who fit into this category. I'm thinking of the fellow from SMU in Dallas who had done everything in the book. You name it, he had been involved in it. Finally he came to realize that, though he was a very sophisticated, handsome, capable, and talented young man who made lots of money in commercials, he was headed for a dead end. He had come to observe that a couple of Christians he knew seemed to know what life was all about and what made them tick. He got to talking with them, then committed his life to Jesus Christ and was revolutionized. His friends on the campus couldn't recognize that he was the same man. They just couldn't believe it, so great was his impact on them.

Christianity Without Christ

On the other hand, I can think of another girl who had been raised in a Christian environment.

She could give you all the answers, recite the catechism, sing the hymns, memorize the verses, and all the rest, but Christianity didn't mean a thing to her. Finally she too came to realize that, even though she had taken communion as a church member, she was not a Christian. Eventually she came to the place of personal commitment to Christ and likewise experienced the same life-transforming revolution that takes place when anybody comes to Christ.

So there is present-day data that we can observe. There are people to whom we can speak, who are alive today, who have had the experience of coming to know Christ personally. We can talk with these people and observe them, thereby validating Christ's claim to deity by firsthand observation of results. This up-to-date personal data buttresses the objective historical facts, and together these two lines of evidence provide overwhelming proof of the truthfulness of Christ's claim to deity.

Proof by Personal Experience

As I mentioned earlier, I had heart surgery in 1954. One of the benefits that came to me from this experience was the awareness of the importance of *personal experience* as the final proof of objective data. When I first discovered that I had a pulmonic condition and that it could possibly be corrected, I read everything about pulmonic ailments that I could get my hands on. I even went down to the library and read the medical journals on the subject. I remember one scholarly, eight-page article which ended, "We can therefore conclude, in the light of data thus far, that there are basically three results of heart surgery: one, marked improvement; two, no improvement; three, death." Well, I thought to myself, that was tremendously profound! I had sort of had that sneaking suspicion myself before I read the article, but it was wonderful to have it confirmed by scientific data!

I got all the information I could about heart surgery. I checked out the surgeon's record and talked to some people who had had this kind of surgery, and I became convinced that the thing for me to do would be to undergo heart surgery. But I still had to exercise faith. My reason took me up to a certain point, but beyond that I had to have faith. I had all the information I could get my hands on, but if that was all the farther I had gone, I would still have that heart condition today. The doctor told me, "If you continue without surgery, in ten to fifteen years your heart will probably enlarge so much that it will collapse."

Faith Beyond Reason

Fortunately, my faith went beyond my reason. I committed my life to that surgeon. If he had gotten the shakes in the middle of that operation, I wouldn't be here today. I exercised faith. It was reasonable faith, since all the data pointed in that direction, but it was nevertheless faith. By the grace of God the operation was a success, but the point is that in many experiences of life faith goes beyond reason.

This is the case in Christianity. Faith is involved in the way we have already described. It's a common experience to us all—faith goes *beyond* reason but not *against* reason. There are many things we may not fully understand, but this does not prevent us from entering into the reality of them.

Is Christianity credible? Yes. Christianity is the most credible experience and life system and key to meaning in the universe that there is. There are some unanswered questions, to be sure, but Christ is very believable. When we exercise faith in Jesus Christ, we find from both the historical and experiential data that He is a worthy object of our faith. As we come to Him we are never disappointed.

7

HOW CAN I BE SURE OF HEAVEN?

How can I be sure of heaven? Men have wrestled with this question since the earliest dawn of history. It's a question that thinking people ultimately come to grips with in terms of their own personal experience. How can I, if there is a life after death, be sure that I am in a positive and meaningful and dynamic relationship with God? How can I be certain that when death comes, when life ceases on this earth, I am in a positive relationship with the Creator of the universe? All through history men have wrestled with this question.

Great Books of the Western World

When I was living in Dallas, Texas, a man visited me one night who turned out to be a salesman for certain great books of the Western world. If you've ever had a visit from one of these book-selling gentlemen, you know that they can go through a very interesting spiel, telling you why you can't live without their books and why you'll maim your children for life if you don't purchase their set, and on and on. He told me I had to buy that night, since the offer expired in three minutes, so I said, "Thank you very much, but goodbye. It's been nice to know you, but I don't appreciate that kind of approach."

But this man was very clever. He circled the field and called back the next morning with the words, "I should have known better. You didn't have a chance to talk to your wife, so the offer has been extended." Well, in the end we bought a set of his books, and I vowed I was going to get my money's worth out of this thing or die in the attempt. In retrospect I think the latter may be truer than the former!

In any case I ended up leafing through the *Syntopicon*, edited by William R. Farmer. It's a very impressive and useful set of books, basically a dictionary of ideas plus an index of all the great thinkers of the Western world. The overview of the book pointed out that more space is devoted to the idea of God than of any of the other 101 ideas in the whole of the *Syntopicon*. More authors are quoted on this particular subject than on any of the other ideas.

The Question of God

Then followed this interesting observation: "The reason for this is obvious: whether one is a believer or an unbeliever, more hangs on life and eternal destiny on the whole question of God and the conclusion to which one comes with reference to this than on any other question of human existence." I thought this was quite an interesting comment, especially since it came from a secular commentary which covered the great ideas with which men are wrestling. I think we would agree, whatever our personal point of view might be, that the concept of God is one of the most crucial questions in all of human experience. We would have to agree that its implications are extremely far-reaching, and that the whole question of certainty of life after death and of relationship with the living God is a crucial issue.

The Question of Heaven

In our consideration of this issue, the first thing to which we need to devote our attention is the whole question of heaven itself. Of course many people in our time say, "Well, heaven is everything that you experience here on earth; all heaven is going to be is what you've got right here." I'm afraid, from my own viewpoint, that this would be a rather dismal prospect for me! If heaven consisted only of life's happy moments on earth, this would be a rather grim experience for a great many people. If we are limited to human speculation about the whole question of God, then we fall prey to all kinds of ideas abounding everywhere. Various people have different ideas about heaven, but the only way in which you and I can know authoritatively whether heaven exists is if God Himself takes the initiative to communicate to you and me what His heaven is really like and how we can enter it and experience a relationship with Him.

Herbert Spencer, the great agnostic philosopher, made the observation about a hundred years ago that a bird has never been known to fly out into space. Therefore, reasoned Spencer, it is obvious that the finite can never penetrate the infinite, and so even if God exists man can never know Him personally or even know anything about the whole question of God's existence.

Now Spencer was right when he observed that birds never fly out into space, but he missed one other possibility, namely, that God the infinite Creator could penetrate our finiteness—that God Himself could take the initiative and come into human experience, thereby revealing to us what He is like and what heaven is like after death on earth. And of course this is exactly what God has done. This is the central thesis of Christianity— that God has penetrated human history in the

Person of Jesus Christ, thereby communicating to us authoritative information about these questions and ending the hopeless confusion that results from human-based philosophic speculations.

The Revelation of God

Jesus Christ claims to be the revelation of God in human personality. When someone asks, "What is God like?" we can respond, "What is Jesus Christ like?" It's interesting to examine what Christ had to say about this whole question of heaven and life after death. He was very explicit about the reality of life after death, and He was very explicit about the fact of heaven and its existence—of the possibility of our being in heaven and of knowing God personally.

Some of the most comforting words in all the Bible occur in the fourteenth chapter of John's Gospel. The first three verses of this chapter say, "Let not your hearts be troubled; believe in God, believe also in me. In my Father's house are many rooms; if it were not so, would I have told you that I go to prepare a place for you? And when I go and prepare a place for you, I will come again and will take you to myself, that where I am you may be also" (John 14:1-3 RSV). Jesus Christ said very clearly to His disciples, "I'm going to prepare a place for you, and because I am going I will be back to receive you to be with me where I am."

John, who was one of Jesus' closest disciples, also wrote some very comforting words in his Book of the Revelation, the last book in the Bible. He says, speaking of heaven and of God, "He will dwell with them . . . . He will wipe away every tear from their eyes, and death shall be no more, neither shall there be mourning nor crying nor pain anymore, for the former things have passed away" (Revelation 21:3, 4 RSV).

Heaven Is a Reality

It is very clear from the words of Jesus Christ, as well as from the words of the rest of the New Testament, that heaven is a reality that can be experienced. Of course there are some things we don't yet know about heaven. Many people have speculated about heaven, giving it dimensions of all kinds as well as various and sundry fantasized ideas. It's interesting to speculate, and I suppose each person is entitled to his speculation, but of course we have to be careful not to attach Biblical authority to our own speculations. But there is no uncertainty at all about the reality of heaven itself. There is no uncertainty at all that heaven is where God is. We don't know where heaven is geographically, but we do know that heaven is where God Himself is. We also know that heaven will be the most wonderful place that can be imagined, the place to which everyone who really understands God looks forward to going with keen anticipation.

The popular misconception about heaven that you often see in cartoons and hear people talk about is that of sitting on a cloud and strumming a harp, so that at the end of two weeks we'll all be bored stiff. That's a great misconception. Heaven will be the most dynamic, expanding experience that can be imagined. It's a place we look forward to not only for rest but for worshipful and stimulating activity.

Sure of Heaven

It is a fact that we as individuals can be sure of going to heaven. Jesus Christ was very explicit about this. Perhaps the most famous of His statements about heaven was to the thief on the cross. We all remember that there were two thieves on the cross, both of them criminals. One of them slandered Jesus Christ with the words, "If he's so great, why doesn't he do something about all this?" The other thief was of a more humble strain, and he realized that Jesus Christ was suffering innocently. So he said to the other thief, "We are suffering the just reward of our deeds." Then he appealed to Jesus Christ to forgive him. Jesus turned to him in words that must have electrified the thief: "Today you will be with me in paradise." That thief had absolute certainty that he would be in the presence of God when death came.

No doubt many of us think it would be wonderful if Christ would speak to us personally those very words, "Today you will be with me in paradise." Actually, Jesus Christ speaks words just as definite as these to us in the twentieth century, and we can be as sure as that thief was that when death comes for us we will be in the presence of God in paradise. In another place Jesus says of His followers (not only of that time but of all times, including us), "I give to my sheep eternal life, and they will never perish, neither shall any man pluck them out of my hand" (John 10:28). In these words Jesus states clearly that every person who trusts Him as the Shepherd-Savior can be sure of eternal life.

Eternal Existence for Everyone

In this passage Jesus also points out something else that is very helpful to notice, namely, that every human being has eternal existence. Those who will be in heaven in direct and vital relationship with the living God through Jesus Christ are spoken of as having eternal life. Those who will be eternally separated from God because of their rebellion and refusal of what God has done for them in Jesus Christ are spoken of as being in eternal death. Yet every human being will exist forever. Eternal life, as Jesus

Christ uses the term, has reference to this relationship of salvation and of assurance of being in the presence of God for all eternity.

Another Biblical evidence of the fact that we can be sure of being in the presence of God comes from 1 John 5:13, in which John, the "beloved Apostle," writes, "These things have I written unto you who believe in the name of the son of God, that you may know that you have eternal life." What a tremendously wonderful thing to know, to be sure of having eternal life! Jesus Christ and the rest of the New Testament writers state very clearly that we can know with absolute certainty that we can be in the presence of God for all eternity. It's not something that we'll discover only at the end of life, breathlessly hoping that we've made it, but rather it's something that you and I can be absolutely certain about right now if we're willing to believe what Jesus Christ is saying to us very clearly.

The Fact of Christ's Death

What is the basis for our certainty of being in heaven after our life on this earth is over? The fundamental basis on which every one of us can be sure that we will be in the presence of God when life ceases on this earth (or if Jesus Christ should return to take those who believe in Him to be with Himself) is the fact of the death of Jesus Christ Himself. Even superficial reading of the

New Testament and of the four Gospels makes it clear that Jesus Christ had a mission when He came into human history.

Christ was born to die, as Dorothy L. Sayers put it in her very famous play performed in England on the BBC. Christ said He came into human history in order to give His life, so that men and women could be reconciled to God and be sure of forgiveness, of eternal life, and of their place in heaven. In one place Jesus said to His listeners, "The Son of man came not to be ministered unto, but to minister, and to give his life a ransom for many" (Mark 10:45). Was Christ's mission successful? Yes. To as many as receive Him, Christ gives eternal life which starts right now and continues on into heaven forever. The believing is up to you.

8

THE PEACE OF CHRIST

God, if we may put it reverently, had a problem.
His creatures, whom He had created perfectly
but with the freedom of choice to obey or disobey
Him, had exercised that freedom of choice,
rebelling against Him and violating His moral
laws. Because God is a Being of infinite holiness,
He couldn't just wave the sins aside and say,
"Well, boys will be boys. We'll forget the whole
thing and everything will be fine; everybody can
come into heaven, and that will be it." God
couldn't do that and still be the moral Upholder
of the universe. You and I would try to impeach a
judge in a court of law today who said to his son
who was brought before him and judged guilty,
"Well, we'll forget it because, after all, he's my
son." No, as the one who upholds the law of the
land, this judge cannot change the law for the

benefit of his son. He must uphold justice even if the person before him is his own son.

God Loves Us

But God also loves us. His infinite holiness makes it impossible for Him to say, "Well, we'll just overlook the whole thing; after all, people are human, so we'll just let them into heaven as they are." Because God loves us, He doesn't want to execute judgment upon us, but how can He manifest His love to us and at the same time uphold His holiness and righteousness? He is torn, so to speak, in the solution of this problem. The answer is, of course, the cross of Jesus Christ. Here God Himself, in the Person of His Son, voluntarily took the sentence of judgment which belonged to you and me, so that now His justice is fully satisfied. Now in love God can freely offer us reconciliation and forgiveness and assurance of life after death.

The Banker and the Judge

There's a sad but true illustration of two men who went to university together in Australia. One ultimately became a banker, and the other became a lawyer and later a judge. Both of the men had brilliant careers, but after about twenty years one of the men was discovered to have embezzled several million dollars. It was not the judge in this case, but the banker, since he was the one who had access to the several million dollars. As circumstances worked out, the case came up before this particular judge who was the college friend of the banker. Of course there was a great deal of speculation in the press as to what would happen. What would this judge do? Would he, because the defendant was his friend, be lenient? Or would he, for fear of criticism, be overly strict and extreme in his judgment of the case?

The case was tried with a packed courtroom, and finally the verdict was brought in. The banker was pronounced guilty. Then came the time for sentencing, and people wondered exactly what would happen. They were shocked when the judge stood and read the maximum possible sentence which could be imposed under that particular law code. It was a fine of one hundred thousand dollars.

After the spectators had gotten over their initial shock, they watched the judge stand up, walk around the bench, take off his robes, and put his arm around his friend with the words, "I have sold my house and every one of my investments, and I will pay this debt for you." The judge had put himself almost to the point of bankruptcy in order to take the place of his friend, to pay the debt which had to be executed if justice were to be carried out. At the same time, he wanted to illustrate his love for his friend whom he had not forgotten, so he himself paid the fine and the sentence. This, I say, is only a very faint illustration of what God has done for us in Jesus Christ. This is the basis on which we can be sure of forgiveness of sin and of eternal life in God's presence in heaven.

Personal Faith in Christ

But there is one other aspect to the assurance of our presence in heaven, and that is faith itself. We must, if we are to be personally sure of being in heaven with God for all eternity, exercise personal faith in Jesus Christ as our own Savior and Lord. As we showed earlier in this book, faith does not create truth. Believing something does not make something true out of something false. Faith simply allows me to experience that which is *already true*. Faith enables me to experience *the reality that already is.* The fact that Jesus Christ died and rose again makes it *possible* for every one of us to be forgiven and reconciled, but to personally experience this relationship with the living God we *must exercise faith* in the Lord Jesus Christ as our personal Savior.

Taking the Vaccine

It's like polio vaccine. We're all tremendously grateful to Dr. Jonas Salk and Dr. Albert Sabin for the tremendous research that they undertook in order to develop the vaccine and the pill which can immunize us against polio. But, you know, the fact that the polio protection is available doesn't mean a thing to you or me unless we have personally taken the vaccine. Potentially, polio can be wiped out, but it doesn't mean a thing to us as individuals until we have experienced the vaccine itself.

That's exactly the way it is with reference to the death of Jesus Christ and the question of assurance of heaven. Christ died for us, so it is *possible* for us to have certainty, but this possibility doesn't mean a thing to us unless we have personally come into vital contact with Jesus Christ Himself. Our certainty of heaven is based on *what God has done for us* rather than on what we do for God. This is a crucial point in the issue of eternal life.

We Have All Sinned

Many people have the mistaken idea that our assurance of eternal life and of heaven is somehow based on what we do for God—the kind of life we live and the good works we perform. They feel that if somehow our good works can outweigh our bad works, there's a good chance we might make it into heaven. The fact of the matter is that if our assurance of heaven is based on the works that you or I do, there is really no chance at all. How do you or I ever know when we've done enough good works to qualify for the presence of God? It's an impossibility, according to Romans 3:23—"All have sinned and come short of the glory of God."

As we saw in one of our earlier discussions, God's standard of behavior is the absolute perfection of Christ Himself. Deep inside we all know we've missed that standard—we've been corrupt in thought and action and word. It is therefore impossible for us to come into the presence of God and to be related to Him on the basis of the life we've lived. It is not a question of *what we do for God*, but of *what God has done for us*.

No Proud Society

If salvation were based on works, heaven would be an intolerably proud society, wouldn't it? If eternal life were based on what we did, we know well enough that we would be insufferably proud, tooting our horns and looking down our noses at those who didn't quite make it. Salvation on this basis would be a contradiction of terms: heaven would be hell with that kind of attitude dominating the place. Paul the Apostle was very explicit on this point in his Letter to the Ephesians. He makes a very clear, straightforward statement when He says, "By grace you have been saved through faith, and this is not your own doing; it is the gift of God—not because of works, lest any man should boast" (Ephesians 2:8, 9 RSV). Works are not the basis on which any of us can be sure of our relationship to God and our place in heaven. If it were, there would be no hope for any of us. Instead, our hope is in what God has done for us, in accepting God at His own word.

Dr. Nicodemus

Nicodemus is one man who didn't understand this truth at first. Nicodemus, as you recall from the third chapter of John's Gospel, was a cultured man, a leader among the Jews, a lawyer and university graduate. he had heard about this Jesus of Nazareth, so he came around one night to see what Christ's teaching was all about. Nicodemus was trying to figure out who Jesus was, so he said, "Rabbi, we know you are a teacher come from God, for no man can do these miracles that you are doing unless God were with him" (John 3:2).

Jesus Christ replied with a very direct statement to Nicodemus: "Except a man be born again, he cannot see the kingdom of God." Nicodemus was a little startled by this statement, since he took it in the physical sense, so he replied, "Well, I don't quite understand that. How can a man be born again when he is old?" He couldn't figure out how we could go through this whole process of physical birth again. Jesus said to him, "Nicodemus, you don't understand;

that which is born of the flesh is flesh and that which is born of the spirit is spirit. Don't be surprised because I say to you that you must be born again."

In other words, cats beget cats, human beings beget human beings, and flesh begets flesh. We need to be born *spiritually* if we are to see the kingdom of God. Jesus continued by pointing out to Nicodemus that even though every human being has *physical* life by virtue of being born into this world, we do not have *spiritual* life because of this physical birth. As a matter of fact, every human being is born spiritually dead because of the separation from God that we were speaking about. The only way we can be sure of entering the kingdom of God is to have a *spiritual birth*, to be born again as Jesus Christ described it to Nicodemus. It's not something that happens to us naturally, but something that happens to us when we make a definite personal transaction with Jesus Christ. Then we are born into *His* family—we become *His* child and we qualify to become a citizen of *His* heaven, of the kingdom of God.

It's Not How We Feel

Our salvation and assurance of heaven, as we have seen, is based on what God has done for us and not on what we do for God. We must also note that eternal life is not based on our feelings. There are some people who say, "Well, I feel like I'm a Christian." And there are others who say, "I don't feel like I'm a Christian." When we wake up in the morning with a headache, and the toast is burned and the scrambled eggs are sort of sour, and we don't feel like much of anything at that time in the morning, our assurance of salvation could be blown to bits if it's based on personal feelings!

No, if we are to be sure of our relationship with God, if we are to be sure of our destiny in heaven, our assurance cannot rest on how we feel but on God's promise of personal relationship through Christ. The permanence of this relationship can be illustrated by marriage. Somebody comes to me, let's say, when I'm speaking in California. I've just had sixteen meetings in three days, and students have been talking to me until four in the morning, and then somebody comes to me and says, "Do you feel married?" Well, I don't feel like much of anything at that point except flopping somewhere. If somebody says to me, "Do you know you're married?" I say, "Sure I know I'm married." I don't feel anything except bone-weariness at that point, but I know I'm married because the certainty of my marriage relationship hinges on the fact that at a particular time and place I committed myself to my wife and she to me—we established a permanent relationship. Our feelings come and go, but the *abiding relationship* is what counts in marriage as well as in salvation.

Fact, Faith, and Feeling

You may have heard the old proverb of Mr. Fact, Mr. Faith, and Mr. Feeling. Mr. Fact, Mr. Faith, and Mr. Feeling were walking along a very narrow wall. As long as Mr. Faith kept his eyes on Mr. Fact, Mr. Feeling followed right along and they made beautiful progress. But every time Mr. Faith turned around and looked at Mr. Feeling, they almost fell off, because they were so paralyzed with fear. They just crept along inch-by-inch out of mortal fear. The moral of the story is that "our feelings will follow our faith in the facts." Our certainty of salvation rests in the fact of what God has done for us in Jesus Christ and the fact of our personal commitment to Jesus Christ. If our faith lies in these facts, we find our feelings following along without difficulty.

No Room for Arrogance

There's another thing we should observe about this question of certainty of being in heaven: when we have achieved the certainty that if death should come to us tonight we would be in the presence of God, this does not mean we are arrogant. Some people are disturbed that anyone should have the audacity to say, "I'm sure I am related to the living God and have eternal life." They misunderstand this person as saying, "I'm a hotshot, and if you were as good a hotshot as I am, you could have this same certainty."

By no means. Our assurance of salvation cannot be based on pride in any way, shape, or form, since our assurance has nothing to do with what *we* have done, but only with what *God has done for us in Jesus Christ*. Basically, the person who says he knows he will be in heaven is simply taking God at His word. He is simply believing that God has spoken the truth, and he is entering into the experiential certainty of God's promise.

No Careless Attitudes

Being sure of our relationship to Jesus Christ and being certain of heaven does not mean that we can develop a careless attitude toward life and sin. I've had people say to me, "Well, if you're sure you have eternal life and will be in the presence of God, that means there's no incentive for you to live a good life. Do you mean to say your sins are forgiven and you're sure of it? Why, you could live as you please. That can't possibly be the way God works." This is an understandable misconception. It would perhaps seem on the surface that this criticism is true—that if a person could be sure of his salvation he would live as he pleased in sin and disobedience.

However, there is one vital and overwhelming fact that is often overlooked: when this relationship with Jesus Christ is established, an internal revolution takes place within the life of the person who encounters Jesus Christ.

A Whole New Creation

The Apostle Paul goes so far as to call this revolution a whole new creation. What happens is that we receive a whole new life. Our whole orientation toward life changes—what we were interested in before, we suddenly lose interest in; spiritual realities that before didn't interest us in the least, we suddenly become vitally interested in. We find that we have a greater sensitivity to sin and rebellion against God than we have ever had before in our lives, and we begin to loathe sin as never before.

Because we love Jesus Christ and recognize what He has done for us by giving His life for us in love, we find that we want to do nothing that will displease or hurt Him. When we become conscious of violating His law or of doing something wrong, it pains us very greatly and we immediately want reconciliation and forgiveness. The key to understanding that we don't just do as we please after we receive the assurance of eternal life is a proper understanding of the new life in Christ, of the revolutionizing experience which makes it impossible to be indifferent to sin.

The Keeper and the Wife

Perhaps this is well illustrated by the difference that takes place in the life of a housekeeper who is hired by a wealthy businessman. He hires her and says, "Now look, I'm paying you a hundred dollars a week, and here's a list of forty things I want you to do. Here's the list, and I'm paying you to do these things." The housekeeper is getting paid to do these things, so she does them.

But now suppose that this housekeeper and this businessman fall in love and are ultimately married. He goes off to work and leaves no list, and his friends say to him, "You're crazy! No list? She'll sit there with her feet up on the table all day long, watching television and eating chocolates. The place will be a shambles. You're crazy. You better get her back on that list." But the businessman replies, "No, you don't understand. I don't need to give her a list. She'll do sixty things with no list." Why? Because the woman is no longer just a hired housekeeper, but is a wife who loves her husband. A whole new relationship has developed, and the list is no longer necessary. The relationship has been transformed by love.

This is precisely what happens in the life of a

person who encounters Jesus Christ as Savior and Lord. The whole relationship is changed, and the believer doesn't need the club of fear anymore. Love is a much stronger incentive than the club of fear; because we love Christ, we are very sensitive to the whole question of disobedience and rebellion.

Relationship Versus Fellowship

One additional observation: if a Christian sins after he has come into this relationship with Jesus Christ, it does not mean that he loses this relationship and it has to be reestablished, but rather, it's the *fellowship and communion within that relationship* that have to be reestablished. Some people are disturbed by thinking that, when they become conscious of having done something wrong after they have come into this relationship with Christ, somehow the relationship needs to be established all over again. But this is not the case.

Again, let's think of marriage as an illustration. Being married is a one-time situation, isn't it? We receive a person into our lives by committing ourselves to that person—a permanent marriage relationship. But suppose a year later we develop marital tensions. Somebody walks into our house and could cut the atmosphere with a knife. Something is wrong somewhere. But do we need to go out and get married again? No. What we need is to have our *fellowship and communion* restored. That will take place only when one or both parties (as the case may require) makes confession and restoration. Then the air is cleared, forgiveness is granted, communication is restored, and communion and fellowship are reestablished. The relationship was always there, but the fellowship and communion needed to be reestablished.

The Permanent Relationship

This is what happens in the life of a Christian. He comes to the place of a onetime commitment to Jesus Christ as Savior and Lord. An internal revolution takes place, in which he now comes to love Christ and becomes very concerned about doing His will. When the believer senses sin or disobedience in his life, it pains him deeply. He doesn't need to have the *relationship* reestablished, but he does need to come to Jesus Christ the moment he is aware of having departed from His will. He needs to confess his sins and ask for the forgiveness which Jesus Christ promises. Then his fellowship and communion will be restored.

False Foundations

When we understand that the issue of certainty of eternal life is based exclusively on the fact of our personal relationship with Jesus Christ as Savior and Lord, we can understand the inadequacy of certain of the bases of assurance that some people are depending on. Heredity, for example, is one false foundation that some people are leaning on. You ask them, "Will you be in heaven?" and they say, "Oh, yes, our family has been Christian for four generations! or "I was born a Christian!" That's like saying to a person, "How long have you been married?" only to have him reply, "Oh, I was born married!" It's an impossibility. Salvation has to be established in personal, individual terms.

Then there are those who think that a particular ritual or a recognized church membership will guarantee their future in heaven. As a friend of mine has observed, a Christian will always go to church, but going to church no more makes a person a Christian or gives him assurance of heaven than going into a garage makes him an automobile. It just doesn't work that way! A Christian will go to church *not* as a means by which to be sure but as an expression of that certainty.

How to Be Sure of Heaven

Every one of us can be absolutely sure that we will be in heaven if we have personally committed ourselves to Jesus Christ in an act of faith. To put it very simply, the way we can answer for ourselves, "Can I be sure of being in heaven?" is by answering the question, "Have I ever personally for myself, specifically and definitely, invited Jesus Christ to come into my life as Savior and Lord?" If I have done that, then on the authority of what God Himself says in His Word I can be absolutely sure of heaven and of an eternity with Jesus Christ. This is the way to be sure of the eternal relationship of love which God offers to me in Jesus Christ.

"JUST LIKE BEING THERE"

The content of this book is also available in tape cassette form, in a convenient protective package. You can bring the vitality and personality of great authors and speakers right into your home, car, study group or church through the magic of modern quality tape cassettes, recorded live before real audiences for your spiritual growth and listening pleasure.

You can make double use of your time, too:
• listen and learn while you drive to and from work
• listen and learn while you work around your home
• listen and learn while you relax at home or on vacation
Use tape cassettes in study groups, in the church, in the home, in youth meetings. You can listen as long as you want—then stop the tape anytime to discuss the speaker's points.